simple
suppers

essential recipes

Publisher's Note:
Raw or semi-cooked eggs should not be consumed by babies, toddlers, pregnant women,
the elderly, or those suffering from a chronic illness.

Recipe Note:
All eggs are large size and all vegetables are medium size, unless otherwise stated.

Publisher and Creative Director: Nick Wells
Project Editor: Catherine Taylor
Photographers: Paul Forrester, Colin Bowling and Stephen Brayne
Home Economists & Stylists: Jaqueline Bellefontaine,
Mandy Phipps, Vicki Smallwood and Penny Stephens
Art Director: Mike Spender
Layout Design: Dave Jones
Digital Design and Production: Chris Herbert and Claire Walker
Proofreader: Julia Rolf

Special thanks to: Polly Prior, Joseph Kelly and Giana Porpiglia.

11 13 15 14 12

1 3 5 7 9 10 8 6 4 2

This edition first published 2011 by
FLAME TREE PUBLISHING
Crabtree Hall, Crabtree Lane
Fulham, London SW6 6TY
United Kingdom

www.flametreepublishing.com

Flame Tree is part of The Foundry Creative Media Co. Ltd

© 2011 this edition The Foundry Creative Media Co. Ltd

ISBN 978-0-85775-155-3

A CIP record for this book is available from the British Library upon request.

Printed in China

simple
suppers

essential recipes

General Editor: Gina Steer

FLAME TREE
PUBLISHING

Contents

Poultry & Meat

Desserts

Hygiene in the Kitchen

It is important to remember that many foods can carry some form of bacteria. In most cases, the worst it will lead to is a bout of food poisoning or gastroenteritis, but this can be serious for certain people. The risk can be reduced or eliminated, however, by good hygiene and proper cooking.

Do not buy food that is past its sell, or pull, date and do not consume food past its expiration date. When buying food, use your eyes and nose. If the food looks tired, limp, or a bad color or it has a rank, acrid, or bad smell, do not buy or eat it under any circumstances.

Dish towels must be washed and changed regularly. Ideally, use disposable cloths, which should be replaced on a daily basis. More durable cloths should be left to soak in bleach, then washed in the washing machine at a high temperature. Keep your hands, cooking utensils, and food preparation surfaces clean and do not let pets climb onto any work counters. Avoid handling food if you have a stomach ache because bacteria can be passed on through food preparation.

Buying

Avoid bulk buying where possible, especially fresh produce. Fresh foods lose their nutritional value rapidly, so buying a little at a time minimizes loss of nutrients. Check that any packaging is intact and not damaged or pierced. Store fresh foods in the refrigerator as soon as possible.

When buying frozen foods, make sure that they are not heavily iced on the outside and that the contents feel completely frozen. Make sure that they have been stored in the cabinet at the correct storage level and the temperature is below -0.4˚F. Pack in cooler bags to transport home and place in the freezer as soon as possible after purchase.

Preparation

Be especially careful when preparing raw meat and fish. A separate cutting board should be used for each, and the knife, board, and your hands should be thoroughly washed before handling or preparing any other food. A variety of good-quality plastic boards come in various designs and colors. This makes differentiating easier and the plastic has the added hygienic advantage of being washable at high temperatures in the dishwasher. If using the board for fish, first wash in cold water, then in hot to prevent odor.

When cooking, be particularly careful to keep cooked and raw food separate to avoid any contamination. It is worth washing all fruits and vegetables regardless of whether they are going to be eaten raw or lightly cooked. This rule should apply even to packages of prewashed herbs and salads.

Do not reheat food more than once. If using a microwave, always check that the food is piping hot all the way through—in theory, the food should reach 158˚F and needs to be cooked at that temperature for at least three minutes to make sure that all bacteria are killed.

All poultry must be thoroughly thawed before using. Remove the food to be thawed from the freezer and place in a shallow dish to contain the juices. Leave the food in the refrigerator until it is completely thawed. A 3-pound whole chicken will take about 26–30 hours to thaw. To speed up the process, immerse the chicken in cold water, making sure that the water is changed regularly. When the pieces can move freely and no ice crystals remain in the cavity, the bird is completely thawed. Once thawed, remove the packaging and pat the chicken dry. Place the chicken in a shallow dish, cover lightly, and store as close to the bottom of the refrigerator as possible. The chicken should be cooked as soon as possible.

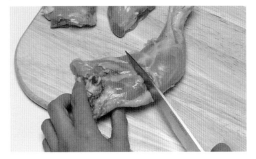

Some foods can be cooked from frozen, including many prepared foods, such as soups, sauces, casseroles, and breads. Where applicable, follow the manufacturers' directions. Vegetables and fruits can also be cooked from frozen, but meats and fish should be thawed first. The only time food can be refrozen is when the food has been thoroughly thawed, then cooked. Once the food has cooled, then it can be frozen again, but it should only be stored for one month.

All poultry and game (except for duck) must be cooked thoroughly. When cooked, the juices will run clear on the thickest part of the bird—the best area to try is usually the thigh. Other meats, such as ground meat and pork, should be cooked all the way through. Fish should turn opaque, be firm in texture, and break easily into large flakes.

When cooking leftovers, make sure they are reheated until piping hot and that any sauce or soup reaches boiling point first.

Storing, Refrigerating, and Freezing

Meat, poultry, fish, seafood, and dairy products should all be refrigerated. The temperature of the refrigerator should be between 34˚F and 41˚F, while the freezer temperature should not rise above -0.4˚F. To ensure the optimum temperature, avoid leaving the door open for long periods. Try not to overstock, because this reduces the airflow inside and, therefore, the effectiveness in cooling the food within.

When refrigerating cooked food, let it cool down quickly and completely before refrigerating. Hot food will raise the temperature of the refrigerator and possibly affect or spoil other food stored in it.

Food should always be covered. Raw and cooked food should be stored in separate parts of the refrigerator. Cooked food should be kept on the top shelves, while raw meat, poultry, and fish should be placed at the bottom to avoid drips and cross-contamination. It is recommended that eggs be refrigerated in order to maintain their freshness and shelf life.

Regularly clean, defrost, and clear out the refrigerator or freezer—it is worth checking the packaging to see exactly how long each product is safe to freeze. Be careful that frozen foods are not kept stored in the freezer for too long. Blanched vegetables can be stored for one month; beef, lamb, poultry, and pork for six months; and unblanched vegetables and fruits in syrup for a year. Oily fish and sausages can be stored for three months. Dairy products can last four to six months, while cakes and pastries can be kept in the freezer for three to six months.

High-Risk Foods

Certain foods carry risks to people who are considered vulnerable, such as the elderly, the ill, pregnant women, babies, young infants, and those people with a chronic illness.

There is a slight chance that some eggs carry the bacteria salmonella. Cook the eggs until both the yolk and the white are firm to eliminate this risk. Pay particular attention to dishes and products incorporating lightly cooked or raw eggs, which should be eliminated from the diet. Hollandaise sauce, mayonnaise, mousses, soufflés, and meringues all use raw or lightly cooked eggs, as do custard-based dishes, ice creams, and sorbets. These are all considered high-risk foods to the vulnerable groups mentioned above.

Certain meats and poultry also carry the potential risk of salmonella and so should be cooked thoroughly until the juices run clear and there is no pinkness left. Unpasteurized products, such as milk, cheese (especially soft cheese), pâté, and meat (both raw and cooked), all have the potential risk of listeria and should be avoided.

When buying seafood, buy from a reputable source that has a high turnover to ensure freshness. Fish should have bright clear eyes, shiny skin, and bright pink or red gills. The fish should feel stiff to the touch, with a slight smell of sea air. The flesh of fish steaks and fillets should be translucent with no signs of discoloration. Mollusks, such as scallops, clams, and mussels, are sold fresh and are still alive. Avoid any that are open or do not close when tapped lightly. In the same way, univalves, such as abalones or periwinkles, should withdraw back into their shells when lightly prodded. When choosing cephalopods, such as squid and octopus, they should have a firm flesh and pleasant sea smell. With all seafood care is required when freezing it. If it has been frozen,

Nutrition: The Role of Essential Nutrients

A healthy and well-balanced diet is the body's primary energy source. In children, it constitutes the building blocks for future health as well as providing a lot of energy. In adults, it encourages self-healing and regeneration within the body. A well-balanced diet will provide the body with all the essential nutrients it needs. This can be achieved by eating a variety of foods, demonstrated in the pyramid below.

FATS

PROTEINS

milk, yogurt,   meat, fish, poultry,
and cheese   eggs, nuts, and beans

FRUIT AND VEGETABLES

STARCHY CARBOHYDRATES

cereals, potatoes, bread, rice, and pasta

FATS

Fats fall into two categories: saturated and unsaturated. Fats are an essential part of the diet; they are a source of energy and provide essential fatty acids and fat-soluble vitamins, but it is very important that a healthy balance is achieved. The right balance should boost the body's immunity to infection and keep muscles, nerves, and arteries in good condition. Saturated fats are of animal origin and can be found in dairy produce, meat, eggs, margarines, and hard white cooking fat (lard) as well as in manufactured products, such as pies, cookies, and cakes. A high intake of saturated fat over many years has been proven to increase heart disease and high blood cholesterol levels and often leads to weight gain. Lowering the amount of saturated fat that we consume is very important, but this does not mean that it is good to consume a lot of other types of fat.

There are two kinds of unsaturated fats: polyunsaturated and monounsaturated. Polyunsaturated fats include safflower, soybean, corn, and sesame oils. The omega-3 oils in polyunsaturated fats have been found to be beneficial to coronary health and can encourage brain growth and development. They are derived from oily fish, such as salmon, mackerel, herring, pilchards, and sardines. It is recommended that we should eat these types of fish at least once a week. Alternative liver oil supplements are also available. The most popular oils that are high in monounsaturates are olive oil, sunflower oil, and peanut oil. Monounsaturated fats are also known to help reduce the levels of cholesterol.

PROTEINS

Composed of amino acids—proteins' building blocks—proteins perform a wide variety of essential functions for the body, including supplying energy and building and repairing tissues. Good sources of proteins are eggs, milk, yogurt, cheese, meat, fish, poultry, eggs, nuts, and beans. (See the Proteins level of the pyramid.) Some of these foods, however, contain saturated fats. To strike a nutritional balance, eat generous amounts of vegetable protein foods, such as soybeans and other beans, lentils, peas, and nuts.

MINERALS

CALCIUM Important for healthy bones and teeth, nerve transmission, muscle contraction, blood clotting, and hormone function. Calcium promotes a healthy heart, improves skin, relieves aching muscles and bones, maintains the correct acid-alkaline balance, and reduces menstrual cramps. Good sources are dairy products, small bones of small fish, nuts, beans, fortified white flours, breads, and green leafy vegetables.

CHROMIUM Balances blood sugar levels, helps to normalize hunger and reduce cravings, improves lifespan, helps protect DNA, and is essential for heart function. Good sources are brewer's yeast, whole-wheat bread, rye bread, oysters, potatoes, green bell peppers, butter, and parsnips.

IODINE Important for the manufacture of thyroid hormones and for normal development. Good sources are seafood, seaweed, milk, and dairy.

IRON As a component of hemoglobin, iron carries oxygen around the body. It is vital for normal growth and development. Good sources are liver, corned beef, red meat, fortified breakfast cereals, beans, green leafy vegetables, egg yolk, and cocoa and cocoa products.

MAGNESIUM Important for efficient functioning of metabolic enzymes and development of the skeleton. Magnesium promotes healthy muscles by helping them to relax and is, therefore, good for PMS. It is also important for heart muscles and the nervous system. Good sources are nuts, green vegetables, meat, cereals, milk, and yogurt.

PHOSPHORUS Forms and maintains bones and teeth, builds muscle tissue, helps maintain pH of the body, and aids metabolism and energy production. Phosphorus is present in almost all foods.

POTASSIUM Enables processing of nutrients; promotes healthy nerves and muscles; maintains fluid balance; helps secretion of insulin for blood sugar control; relaxes muscles; maintains heart functioning; and stimulates digestive movement. Good sources are fruit, vegetables, milk, and bread.

SELENIUM Antioxidant properties help to protect against free radicals and carcinogens. Selenium reduces inflammation, stimulates the immune system, promotes a healthy heart, and helps vitamin E's action. Necessary for the male reproductive system and for metabolism. Good sources are tuna, liver, kidney, meat, eggs, cereals, nuts, and dairy products.

SODIUM Important in helping to control body fluid, preventing dehydration. Sodium is involved in muscle and nerve function and helps move nutrients into cells. All foods are good sources. Processed, pickled, and salted foods are richest in sodium but should be eaten in moderation.

ZINC Important for metabolism and healing; aids ability to cope with stress; promotes a healthy nervous system and brain, especially in the growing fetus; aids bone and teeth formation; and is essential for energy. Good sources are liver, meat, beans, whole-grain cereals, nuts, and oysters.

VITAMINS

VITAMIN A Important for cell growth and development and for the formation of visual pigments in the eye. Vitamin A comes in two forms: retinol and beta-carotene. Retinol is found in liver, meat, and whole milk. Beta-carotene is a powerful antioxidant and is found in red and yellow fruits and vegetables, such as carrots, mangoes, and apricots.

VITAMIN B1 (THIAMINE) Important in releasing energy from carbohydrate-containing foods. Good sources are yeast and yeast products, bread, fortified breakfast cereals, and potatoes.

VITAMIN B2 (RIBOFLAVIN) Important for metabolism of proteins, fats, and carbohydrates to produce energy. Good sources are meat, yeast extracts, fortified breakfast cereals, and milk and its products.

VITAMIN B3 (NIACIN) Required for the metabolism of food into energy. Good sources are milk, fortified cereals, beans, meat, poultry, and eggs.

VITAMIN B5 (PANTOTHENIC ACID) Important for the metabolism of food and energy production. All foods are good sources but especially fortified breakfast cereals, whole-grain bread, and dairy products.

VITAMIN B6 Important for metabolism of protein and fat. Vitamin B6 may also be involved in the regulation of sex hormones. Good sources are liver, fish, pork, soybeans, and peanuts.

BIOTIN (VITAMIN B7) Important for metabolism of fatty acids. Good sources are liver, kidney, eggs, and nuts.

FOLIC ACID (VITAMIN B9) Essential for brain and nerve function, for utilizing protein, and for red blood cell formation. It is also critical during pregnancy for the baby's brain and nerve development. Good sources are whole-grain and fortified cereals, green leafy vegetables, oranges, and liver.

VITAMIN B12 Important for the production of red blood cells and DNA. It is vital for growth and the nervous system. Good sources are meat, fish, eggs, poultry, and milk.

VITAMIN C Important for healing wounds and the formation of collagen, which keeps skin and bones strong. It is an important antioxidant. Good sources are fruits, especially berries, and vegetables.

VITAMIN D Important for absorption and handling of calcium to help build bone strength. Good sources are oily fish, eggs, whole milk and milk products, margarine, and, of course, sufficient exposure to sunlight, because vitamin D is made in the skin.

VITAMIN E Important as an antioxidant vitamin helping to protect cell membranes from damage. Good sources are vegetable oils, margarines, seeds, nuts, and green vegetables.

VITAMIN K Important for controlling blood clotting. Good sources are cauliflower, Brussels sprouts, lettuce, cabbage, beans, broccoli, peas, asparagus, potatoes, corn oil, tomatoes, and milk.

CARBOHYDRATES

Carbohydrates are an energy source and come in two forms: starch and sugar. Starch carbohydrates are also known as complex carbohydrates and they include all cereals, potatoes, breads, rice, and pasta. Eating whole-grain varieties of these foods also provides fiber. Diets high in fiber are believed to be beneficial in helping to prevent bowel cancer and keep cholesterol down. Sugar carbohydrates—also known as fast-release carbohydrates because they provide a quick fix of energy—include sugar and sugar-sweetened products. Other sugars are lactose (from milk) and fructose (from fruit).

Soups & Salads

Accompanied by crusty bread or croutons, soup can make for a satisfying meal. Try Italian Bean Soup for a quick week-night pick-me-up, or how about Potato, Leek & Rosemary Soup for a twist on an old favorite? Salads provide a feast for the eyes as well as the palate: Warm Noodle Salad with Sesame & Peanut Dressing is a good winter warmer, while the Bulgur Wheat Salad with Minty Lemon Dressing is a perfect summer dish.

Tomato & Basil Soup

1 Preheat the oven to 400°F. Evenly spread the tomato halves and unpeeled garlic in a single layer in a large roasting pan.

2 Mix the oil and vinegar together. Drizzle over the tomatoes and sprinkle with the dark brown sugar.

3 Roast the tomatoes in the preheated oven for 20 minutes until tender and lightly charred in places.

4 Remove from the oven and allow to cool slightly. When cool enough to handle, squeeze the softened flesh of the garlic from the papery skin. Place with the charred tomatoes in a strainer over a saucepan.

5 Press the garlic and tomato through the strainer with the back of a wooden spoon.

6 When all the flesh has been strained, add the tomato paste and the vegetable stock to the pan. Heat gently, stirring occasionally.

7 In a small bowl beat the yogurt and basil together, and season to taste with salt and pepper. Stir the basil yogurt into the soup. Garnish with basil leaves and serve immediately.

Ingredients   SERVES 4

7 medium, ripe tomatoes, cut in half
2 garlic cloves
1 tsp. olive oil
1 tbsp. balsamic vinegar
1 tbsp. dark brown sugar
1 tbsp. tomato paste
$1^1/_4$ cups vegetable stock
6 tbsp. low-fat plain yogurt
2 tbsp. freshly chopped basil
salt and freshly ground black pepper
small basil leaves, to garnish

Tasty tip

Use the sweetest type of tomatoes available, as it makes a big difference to the flavor of the soup. Many supermarkets now stock special tomatoes, grown slowly and matured for longer on the vine to give them an intense flavor. If these are unavailable, add a little extra sugar to bring out the flavor.

Curried Parsnip Soup

1 In a small skillet, fry the cumin and coriander seeds over a moderately high heat for 1–2 minutes. Shake the skillet during cooking until the seeds are lightly toasted.

2 Set aside until cooled. Place the toasted seeds in a mortar and grind with a pestle.

3 Heat the oil in a saucepan. Cook the onion until softened and starting to turn golden

4 Add the garlic, turmeric, chili powder, and cinnamon stick to the pan. Continue to cook for an additional minute.

5 Add the parsnips and stir well. Pour in the stock and bring to a boil. Cover and simmer for 15 minutes or until the parsnips are cooked.

6 Allow the soup to cool. Once cooled, remove the cinnamon stick and discard.

7 Blend the soup in a food processor until very smooth. Transfer to a saucepan and reheat gently. Season to taste with salt and pepper. Garnish with fresh cilantro leaves, and serve immediately with yogurt.

Ingredients   SERVES 4

1 tsp. cumin seeds
2 tsp. coriander seeds
1 tsp. oil
1 onion, peeled and chopped
1 garlic clove, peeled and crushed
$^1/_2$ tsp. turmeric
$^1/_4$ tsp. chili powder
1 cinnamon stick
2 cups peeled and chopped parsnips
4 cups vegetable stock
salt and freshly ground black pepper
fresh cilantro leaves, to garnish
2–3 tbsp. low-fat plain yogurt,
   to serve

Food fact

Parsnips vary in color from pale yellow to a creamy white. They are at their best when they are the size of a large carrot. If larger, remove the central core, which can be woody.

Potato, Leek & Rosemary Soup

1 Melt the butter in a large saucepan, add the leeks, and cook gently for 5 minutes, stirring frequently. Remove 1 tablespoon of the cooked leeks and set aside for garnishing.

2 Add the potatoes, vegetable stock, rosemary sprigs, and milk. Bring to a boil, then reduce the heat, cover, and simmer gently for 20–25 minutes until the vegetables are tender.

3 Cool for 10 minutes. Discard the rosemary, then pour into a food processor or blender, and blend well to form a smooth-textured soup.

4 Return the soup to the cleaned saucepan and stir in the chopped parsley and crème fraîche. Season to taste with salt and pepper. If the soup is too thick, stir in a little more milk or water. Reheat gently, without boiling, then ladle into warm soup bowls. Garnish the soup with the set-aside leeks and serve immediately with whole-wheat rolls.

Ingredients   SERVES 4

4 tbsp. butter
1 lb. leeks, trimmed and finely sliced
4 cups peeled and roughly
   chopped potatoes
$3^3/_4$ cups vegetable stock
4 fresh rosemary sprigs
2 cups whole milk
2 tbsp. freshly chopped parsley
2 tbsp. crème fraîche
salt and freshly ground black pepper
whole-wheat rolls, to serve

Tasty tip

This rosemary-scented version of vichyssoise is equally delicious served cold. Allow the soup to cool before covering, then chill in the refrigerator for at least 2 hours. The soup will thicken as it chills, so you may need to thin it to the desired consistency with more milk or stock and season before serving. It is important to use fresh rosemary rather than dried for this recipe.

Cream of Pumpkin Soup

1 Cut the peeled and seeded pumpkin flesh into 1-inch cubes. Heat the olive oil in a large saucepan and cook the pumpkin for 2–3 minutes, coating it completely with oil. Chop the onion and leek finely, and dice the carrot and celery stalks.

2 Add the vegetables to the saucepan with the garlic and cook, stirring, for 5 minutes or until they have begun to soften. Cover the vegetables with the water and bring to a boil. Season with plenty of salt, pepper, and the grated nutmeg, then cover and simmer for 15–20 minutes until all of the vegetables are tender.

3 When the vegetables are tender, remove from the heat, cool slightly, then pour into a food processor or blender. Blend to form a smooth paste, then pass through a strainer into a clean saucepan.

4 Adjust the seasoning to taste and add all but 2 tablespoons of the cream and enough water to obtain the correct consistency. Bring the soup to boiling point, add the cayenne pepper, and serve immediately swirled with cream and accompanied by warm herb bread.

Ingredients   SERVES 4

2 lbs. pumpkin flesh (after peeling
   and discarding the seeds)
$1/4$ cup olive oil
1 large onion, peeled
1 leek, trimmed
1 carrot, peeled
2 celery stalks
4 garlic cloves, peeled and crushed
6 cups water
salt and freshly ground black pepper
$1/4$ tsp. freshly grated nutmeg
$2/3$ cup light cream
$1/4$ tsp. cayenne pepper
warm herb bread, to serve

Food fact

If you cannot find pumpkin, try replacing it with squash. Butternut or acorn squash would both make suitable substitutes. Avoid spaghetti squash, which gets too soft when cooked.

Tuna Chowder

1 Heat the oil in a large, heavy saucepan. Add the onion and celery, and gently cook for about 5 minutes, stirring from time to time until the onion is softened.

2 Stir in the flour and cook for about 1 minute to thicken.

3 Take the saucepan off the heat and gradually pour in the milk, stirring throughout.

4 Add the tuna and its liquid, the drained corn kernels, and the freshly chopped thyme.

5 Mix gently, then bring to a boil. Cover with a lid and simmer for 5 minutes.

6 Remove the saucepan from the heat and season to taste with salt and pepper.

7 Sprinkle the chowder with the cayenne pepper and chopped parsley. Divide among soup bowls and serve immediately.

Ingredients   SERVES 4

2 tsp. oil
1 onion, peeled and finely chopped
2 sticks of celery, trimmed
   and finely sliced
1 tbsp. all-purpose flour
$2^{1}/_{2}$ cups nonfat milk
7oz. canned tuna in water
11oz. canned corn kernels, drained
2 tsp. freshly chopped thyme
salt and freshly ground black pepper
pinch cayenne pepper
2 tbsp. freshly chopped parsley

Tasty tip

This creamy soup also works well using equivalent amounts of canned crabmeat instead of the tuna. For a contrasting taste and to enhance the delicate creaminess of this soup, add a spoonful of low-fat sour cream to the top of the soup. Sprinkle with cayenne pepper, and then garnish with a few chopped chives.

Italian Bean Soup

1 Heat the oil in a large saucepan. Add the leek, garlic, and oregano, and cook for 5 minutes, stirring occasionally.

2 Stir in the green beans and the lima beans. Sprinkle in the pasta and pour in the stock.

3 Bring the stock mixture to a boil, then reduce the heat to a simmer. Cook for 12–15 minutes until the vegetables are tender and the pasta tender but still firm to the bite. Stir occasionally.

4 In a heavy skillet, fry the tomatoes over a high heat until they soften and the skins begin to blacken.

5 Gently crush the tomatoes in the skillet with the back of a spoon, and add to the soup.

6 Season to taste with salt and pepper. Stir in the shredded basil.

Ingredients
SERVES 4

2 tsp. olive oil
1 leek, washed and chopped
1 garlic clove, peeled and crushed
2 tsp. dried oregano
$^3/_4$ cup bite-size trimmed
    green beans
14oz. canned lima beans, drained
    and rinsed
$^3/_4$ cup small pasta shapes
4 cups vegetable stock
8 cherry tomatoes
salt and freshly ground black pepper
3 tbsp. freshly torn basil

Tasty tip

This soup will taste even better the day after it has been made. Make the soup the day before you intend serving it and add a little extra stock when reheating.

Carrot & Ginger Soup

1 Preheat the oven to 350°F. Coarsely chop the bread. Dissolve the yeast extract in 2 tablespoons of warm water, and mix with the bread.

2 Spread the bread cubes over a lightly greased baking sheet and cook for 20 minutes, turning halfway through. Remove from the oven and set aside.

3 Heat the oil in a large saucepan. Gently cook the onion and garlic for 3–4 minutes.

4 Stir in the ground ginger and cook for 1 minute to release the flavor. Add the chopped carrots, then stir in the stock and the fresh ginger. Simmer gently for 15 minutes.

5 Remove from the heat and allow to cool slightly. Blend until smooth, then season to taste with salt and pepper. Stir in the lemon juice. Garnish with the chives and lemon zest, and serve immediately.

Ingredients   SERVES 4

4 slices of bread, crusts removed
1 tsp. yeast extract
2 tsp. olive oil
1 onion, peeled and chopped
1 garlic clove, peeled and crushed
$\frac{1}{2}$ tsp. ground ginger
$2\frac{1}{2}$ cups peeled and chopped carrots
4 cups vegetable stock
1-in. piece ginger, peeled and
    finely grated
salt and freshly ground black pepper
1 tbsp. lemon juice

To garnish:

chives
lemon zest

Tasty tip

This soup would be delicious for special occasions if served with a spoonful of lightly whipped cream or low-fat crème fraîche.

Chinese Salad with Soy & Ginger Dressing

1   Rinse and finely shred the Chinese cabbage and place in a serving dish.

2   Slice the water chestnuts into small slivers and cut the scallions diagonally into 1-inch lengths, then split lengthwise into thin strips.

3   Cut the tomatoes in half, then slice each half into three wedges, and set aside.

4   Simmer the snow peas in boiling water for 2 minutes until beginning to soften, drain, and cut in half diagonally.

5   Arrange the water chestnuts, scallions, snow peas, tomatoes, and bean sprouts on top of the shredded Chinese cabbage. Garnish with the freshly chopped cilantro.

6   Make the dressing by whisking all the ingredients together in a small bowl until mixed thoroughly. Serve with the bread and the salad.

Ingredients   SERVES 4

1 head Chinese cabbage
7oz. canned water chestnuts, drained
6 scallions, trimmed
4 ripe but firm cherry tomatoes
1 cup snow peas
$^{3}/_{4}$ cup bean sprouts
2 tbsp. freshly chopped cilantro

For the dressing:

2 tbsp. corn oil
4 tbsp. light soy sauce
1-in. piece ginger, peeled and grated
2 tbsp. lemon zest
1 tbsp. lemon juice
salt and freshly ground black pepper
crusty white bread, to serve

Warm Noodle Salad with Sesame & Peanut Dressing

1 Place the peanut butter, 4 tablespoons of the sesame oil, the soy sauce, vinegar, and ginger in a food processor. Blend until smooth, then stir in $\frac{1}{3}$ cup hot water, and blend again. Pour in the cream, and blend briefly until smooth. Pour the dressing into a jug and set aside.

2 Bring a saucepan of lightly salted water to a boil, add the noodles and bean sprouts, and cook for 4 minutes or according to the package directions. Drain, rinse under cold running water, and drain again. Stir in the remaining sesame oil, and keep warm.

3 Bring a saucepan of lightly salted water to a boil, and add the baby corn, carrots, and snow peas, and cook for 3–4 minutes until just tender but still crisp. Drain and cut the snow peas in half. Slice the baby corn (if very large) into two or three pieces, and arrange on a warmed serving dish with the noodles. Add the cucumber strips and scallions. Spoon over a little of the dressing, and serve immediately with the remaining dressing.

Ingredients　　　SERVES 4–6

$\frac{1}{2}$ cup smooth peanut butter

6 tbsp. sesame oil

3 tbsp. light soy sauce

2 tbsp. red wine vinegar

1 tbsp. freshly shredded ginger

2 tbsp. heavy cream

8-oz. pack Chinese fine egg noodles

2 cups bean sprouts

$\frac{1}{2}$ lb. baby corn

1 carrot, peeled and thinly sliced

1 cup snow peas

$\frac{1}{2}$ cucumber, cut into thin strips

3 scallions, trimmed and
　finely shredded

Bulgur Wheat Salad with Minty Lemon Dressing

1 Place the bulgur in a large saucepan and cover with boiling water. Simmer for about 10 minutes, then drain thoroughly and turn into a serving bowl.

2 Cut the cucumber into small dice, chop the shallots finely, and set aside. Steam the corn over a saucepan of boiling water for 10 minutes or until tender. Drain and slice into thick chunks.

3 Cut a cross on the top of each tomato, and place in boiling water until their skins start to peel away.

4 Remove the skins and the seeds, and cut the tomatoes into small dice.

5 Make the dressing by briskly whisking all the ingredients in a small bowl until mixed well.

6 When the bulgur has cooled a little, add all the prepared vegetables and stir in the dressing. Season to taste with salt and pepper, and serve.

Ingredients SERVES 4

$^2/_3$ cup bulgur
4-in. piece cucumber
2 shallots, peeled
1 cup baby corn
3 ripe but firm tomatoes

For the dressing:

1 tbsp. lemon rind
3 tbsp. lemon juice
3 tbsp. freshly chopped mint
2 tbsp. freshly chopped parsley
1–2 tsp. honey
2 tbsp. corn oil
salt and freshly ground black pepper

Food fact

This dish is loosely based on the Middle Eastern dish tabbouleh, a type of salad in which all the ingredients are mixed together and served cold.

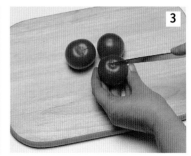

Mixed Salad with Anchovy Dressing & Ciabatta Croutons

1 Divide the endive and chicory into leaves and set aside some of the larger ones. Arrange the smaller leaves in a wide salad bowl.

2 Cut the fennel bulb in half from the stalk to the root end, then cut across in fine slices. Quarter the artichokes, then quarter and slice the cucumber and halve the tomatoes. Add to the salad bowl with the olives.

3 To make the dressing, drain the anchovies and put in a blender with the mustard, garlic, olive oil, lemon juice, 2 tablespoons of hot water, and black pepper. Mix together until smooth and thickened.

4 To make the croutons, cut the bread into $1/_2$-inch cubes. Heat the oil in a skillet, add the bread cubes, and cook for 3 minutes, turning frequently until golden. Remove and drain on absorbent paper towels.

5 Drizzle half the anchovy dressing over the prepared salad and toss to coat. Arrange the endive and chicory leaves around the edge, then drizzle over the remaining dressing. Sprinkle with the croutons and serve immediately.

Ingredients   SERVES 4

1 small head endive
1 small head chicory
1 fennel bulb
14oz. canned artichokes, drained
    and rinsed
$1/_2$ cucumber
1 cup cherry tomatoes
$1/_2$ cup ripe olives

For the anchovy dressing:

2oz. canned anchovy fillets
1 tsp. mustard
1 small garlic clove, peeled and crushed
4 tbsp. olive oil
1 tbsp. lemon juice
freshly ground black pepper

For the ciabatta croutons:

2 thick slices ciabatta or
    similar-style bread
2 tbsp. olive oil

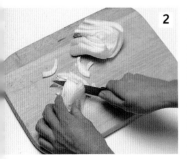

Tortellini & Summer Vegetable Salad

1. Bring a large pan of lightly salted water to a rolling boil. Add the tortellini and cook according to the package directions until tender but still firm to the bite.

2. Using a large slotted spoon, transfer the tortellini to a colander to drain. Rinse under cold running water and drain again. Transfer to a large bowl and toss with 2 tablespoons of the olive oil.

3. Return the pasta water to a boil and drop in the green beans and broccoli florets; blanch them for 2 minutes or until just beginning to soften. Drain, then rinse under cold running water and drain again thoroughly. Add the vegetables to the tortellini.

4. Add the bell pepper, onion, artichoke hearts, capers, and olives to the bowl; stir lightly.

5. Whisk together the vinegar, mustard, and brown sugar in a bowl, and season to taste with salt and pepper. Slowly whisk in the remaining olive oil to form a thick, creamy dressing. Pour over the tortellini and vegetables, add the chopped basil or parsley, and stir until lightly coated. Transfer to a shallow serving dish or salad bowl. Garnish with the hard-boiled egg quarters and serve.

Ingredients
SERVES 6

12 oz. mixed green and plain cheese-filled fresh tortellini

$^2/_3$ cup extra-virgin olive oil

$1^1/_2$ cups trimmed fine green beans

6 oz. broccoli florets

1 yellow or red bell pepper, deseeded and thinly sliced

1 red onion, peeled and sliced

6-oz. jar marinated artichoke hearts, drained and halved

2 tbsp. capers

$^1/_2$ cup dry-cured pitted ripe olives

3 tbsp. raspberry or balsamic vinegar

1 tbsp. Dijon mustard

1 tsp. soft brown sugar

salt and freshly ground black pepper

2 tbsp. freshly chopped basil or Italian flat-leaf parsley

2 quartered hard-boiled eggs, to garnish

Helpful hint
Ordinary small olives can be used instead.

Panzanella

1 Leave the crusts on on the bread. Add 1 teaspoon of red wine vinegar to a pitcher of ice water, put the slices of bread in a bowl, and pour over the water. Make sure the bread is covered completely. Allow to soak for 3–4 minutes until just soft.

2 Remove the soaked bread from the water and squeeze it gently, first with your hands, and then in a clean dishtowel, to remove any excess water. Put the bread on a large plate, cover with a piece of plastic wrap, and chill in the refrigerator for about 1 hour.

3 Meanwhile, beat together the olive oil, the remaining red wine vinegar, and lemon juice in a large serving bowl. Add the garlic and onion, and stir to coat well.

4 Halve the cucumber and remove the seeds. Dice both the cucumber and tomatoes. Add, along with the olives, to the garlic and onions. Tear the bread into bite-size chunks and add to the bowl, along with the fresh basil leaves. Toss, and serve immediately with a grinding of sea salt and black pepper.

Ingredients   SERVES 4

loaf day-old Italian bread, about 9
    thick slices
1 tbsp. red wine vinegar
4 tbsp. olive oil
1 tsp. lemon juice
1 small garlic clove, peeled and
    finely chopped
1 red onion, peeled and finely sliced
1 cucumber, peeled
2 medium ripe tomatoes, seeded
$^3/_4$ cup pitted ripe olives
about 20 basil leaves, coarsely torn,
    or left whole if small
sea salt and freshly ground
    black pepper

Tasty tip

Choose an open-textured Italian bread, such as ciabatta, for this classic Tuscany salad. Look in your local delicatessen for different flavored marinated olives. Try chili and garlic, or basil, garlic, and orange.

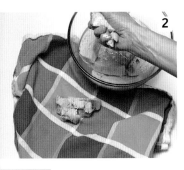

Light Bites

Perfect for a weekday supper with friends or simply when a large meal is not required, this array of dishes is big on flavor without being too rich and filling. Roasted Eggplant Dip with Pita Strips is great for a quick snack, while Thai Fish Cakes or Corn Fritters with Hot & Spicy Relish make for something delectably different.

Roasted Eggplant Dip with Pita Strips

1 Preheat the oven to 350°F. On a chopping board, cut the pita breads into strips, and spread in a single layer onto a large baking sheet.

2 Cook in the preheated oven for 15 minutes or until golden brown and crisp. Allow to cool on a wire rack.

3 Trim the eggplants, rinse lightly, and set aside. Heat a griddle pan until almost smoking. Cook the eggplants and garlic for about 15 minutes.

4 Turn the eggplants frequently until very tender, with wrinkled and charred skins. Remove from the heat. Let cool.

5 When the eggplants are cool enough to handle, cut in half, and scoop out the cooked flesh and place in a food processor.

6 Squeeze the softened garlic flesh from the papery skin, and add to the eggplant in the food processor.

7 Blend the eggplant and garlic until smooth, then add the sesame oil, lemon juice, and cumin, and blend again to mix.

8 Season to taste with salt and pepper, stir in the parsley, and serve with the pita strips and mixed lettuce leaves.

Ingredients SERVES 4

4 pita breads
2 large eggplants
1 garlic clove, peeled
$1/4$ tsp. sesame oil
1 tbsp. lemon juice
$1/2$ tsp. cumin
salt and freshly ground
   black pepper
2 tbsp. freshly chopped parsley
fresh lettuce leaves, to serve

Food fact

This dish is a variation on the traditional Arabic dish known as baba ghanouj, which translates to "spoiled old man." As well as being great with pita strips or grissini, this dish is fantastic as a side dish when served hot.

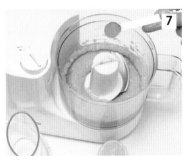

Potato Skins

1 Preheat the oven to 400˚F. Scrub the potatoes, then prick a few times with a fork or skewer and place directly on the top shelf of the oven. Bake in the preheated oven for at least 1 hour until tender. The potatoes are cooked when they yield gently to the pressure of your hand.

2 Set the potatoes aside until cool enough to handle, then cut in half and scoop the flesh into a bowl and set aside. Preheat the broiler, and line the pan with aluminum foil.

3 Mix together the oil and paprika, and use half to brush the outside of the potato skins. Place on the foil-lined pan under the preheated broiler, and cook for 5 minutes or until crisp, turning as necessary.

4 Heat the remaining paprika-flavored oil and gently fry the pancetta until crisp. Add to the potato flesh along with the cream, blue cheese, and parsley. Halve the potato skins, and fill with the blue-cheese filling. Return to the oven for an additional 15 minutes to heat through. Sprinkle with a little more paprika, and serve immediately with mayonnaise, sweet chile sauce, and a green salad.

Ingredients   SERVES 4

4 large baking potatoes
2 tbsp. olive oil
2 tsp. paprika
$^3/_4$ cup roughly chopped pancetta
  or bacon
6 tbsp. heavy cream
$^1/_3$ cup gorganzola
1 tbsp. freshly chopped parsley

To serve:
mayonnaise
sweet chili dipping sauce
tossed green salad

Food fact
A popular Italian cheese produced in Lombardy, Gorgonzola was first made over 1100 years ago, in the village of the same name, near Milan. It is made from pasteurized cow's milk and allowed to ripen for at least 3 months, giving it a rich, but not overpowering, flavor. Unlike most blue cheeses, it has a greater concentration of veining toward the center of the cheese.

Thai Fish Cakes

1 Preheat the oven to 375°F. Place the chile pepper, cilantro, garlic, green onions, and lemon grass in a food processor and blend together.

2 Pat the shrimp and cod dry with a paper towel.

3 Add to the food processor and blend until the mixture is roughly chopped.

4 Season to taste with salt and pepper and blend to mix.

5 Dampen your hands, then shape heaped tablespoons of the mixture into 12 little patties.

6 Place the patties on a lightly oiled baking sheet and cook in the preheated oven for 12–15 minutes, until piping hot and cooked through. Turn the patties over halfway through the cooking time.

7 Serve the fish cakes immediately with the sweet chili sauce for dipping.

Ingredients SERVES 4

1 red chile pepper, deseeded
    and roughly chopped
4 tbsp. roughly chopped fresh cilantro
1 garlic clove, peeled and crushed
2 green onions, trimmed
    and roughly chopped
1 lemon grass, outer
    leaves discarded and
    roughly chopped
3 oz shrimp, thawed if frozen
10 oz cod fillet, skinned, bones
    removed, and cubed
salt and freshly ground black pepper
sweet chili pepper dipping sauce,
    to serve

Tasty tip

A horseradish accompaniment could be used in place of the sweet chili sauce. Mix together 2 tablespoons of grated horseradish (from a jar) with 3 tablespoons each of Greek yogurt and low-calorie mayonnaise. Add 3 finely chopped spring onions, a squeeze of lime and salt and pepper to taste.

Hot Shrimp with Prosciutto

1 Preheat oven to 350°F. Slice the cucumber and tomatoes thinly, then arrange on four large plates and reserve. Peel the shrimp, leaving the tail shell intact, and remove the thin black vein running down the back.

2 Whisk together 4 tablespoons of the olive oil, garlic, and chopped parsley in a small bowl, and season to taste with plenty of salt and pepper. Add the shrimp to the mixture and stir until they are well coated. Remove the shrimp, then wrap each one in a piece of Parma ham and secure with a toothpick.

3 Place the prepared shrimp on a lightly oiled baking sheet or dish with the slices of bread and cook in the preheated oven for 5 minutes.

4 Remove the shrimp from the oven and spoon the wine over the shrimp and bread. Return to the oven and cook for a further 10 minutes, until piping hot.

5 Carefully remove the toothpicks and arrange three shrimp rolls on each slice of bread. Place on top of the sliced cucumber and tomatoes and serve immediately.

Ingredients   SERVES 4

$^1/_2$ cucumber, peeled if preferred

4 ripe tomatoes

12 large, raw shrimp

6 tbsp. olive oil

4 garlic cloves, peeled and crushed

4 tbsp. freshly chopped parsley

salt and freshly ground black pepper

6 slices of Parma ham or prosciutto, cut in half

4 slices flat Italian bread

4 tbsp. dry white wine

Helpful hint

The black intestinal vein needs to be removed from raw shrimp because it can cause a bitter flavor. Remove the shell, then using a small, sharp knife, make a cut along the center back of the shrimp and open out the flesh. Using the tip of the knife, remove the thread that lies along the length of the shrimp, and discard.

Fish Puff Tart

1 Preheat the oven to 425°F. On a lightly floured surface, roll out the pastry into an 8 x 10 inch rectangle.

2 Draw a 7 x 9 inch rectangle in the center of the pastry, to form a 1-inch border. (Be careful not to cut through the pastry.)

3 Lightly cut crisscross patterns in the border of the pastry with a knife.

4 Place the fish on a chopping board, and with a sharp knife, skin the cod and smoked haddock. Cut into thin slices.

5 Spread the pesto evenly over the bottom of the pastry shell with the back of a spoon.

6 Arrange the fish, tomatoes, and cheese in the pastry shell, and brush the pastry with the beaten egg.

7 Bake the tart in the preheated oven for 20–25 minutes until the pastry is well risen, puffed, and golden brown. Garnish with the chopped parsley and serve immediately.

Ingredients   SERVES 4

$^3/_4$ lb. prepared puff pastry, thawed
   if frozen
5 oz. fresh cod
5 oz. smoked haddock
1 tbsp. pesto sauce
2 tomatoes, sliced
4 oz. goat cheese, sliced
1 large egg, beaten
freshly chopped parsley, to garnish

Food fact

The Scottish name for smoked haddock is finnan haddie, named after the Scottish fishing village of Findon, near Aberdeen. Smoked haddock has been a favorite breakfast dish in Findon and the rest of Scotland for many years. Although this type of fish was traditionally caught and smoked (sometimes over peat fires) in Scotland, today the fish is produced in New England and other Eastern coastal states of America.

2

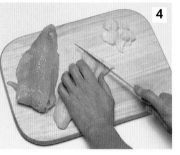

4

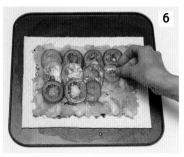

6

Chinese Omelet

1 Lightly rinse the bean sprouts, then place in the top of a bamboo steamer with the carrots. Add the grated ginger and soy sauce. Set the steamer over a pan or wok half-filled with gently simmering water, and steam for 10 minutes or until the vegetables are tender but still crisp. Set aside and keep warm.

2 Whisk the eggs in a bowl until frothy, and season to taste with salt and pepper. Heat an 8-in. omelet pan or skillet, add the sesame oil, and when very hot, pour in the beaten eggs. Whisk the eggs around with a fork, then allow them to cook and start to set. When the surface starts to bubble, lift the edges and tilt the pan to allow the uncooked egg to run underneath.

3 Spoon the bean sprout and carrot mixture over the top of the omelet and allow it to cook a little longer. When it has set, slide the omelet onto a warmed serving dish, and carefully roll up. Serve immediately with a tossed green salad, rice, and extra soy sauce.

Ingredients SERVES 1

1 cup bean sprouts
1 small carrot, peeled and thinly sliced
$1/2$-in. piece ginger, peeled and finely shredded
1 tsp. soy sauce
2 extra-large eggs
salt and freshly ground black pepper
1 tbsp. dark sesame oil

To serve:

tossed green salad
freshly cooked rice, or special fried rice, if liked
soy sauce

Tasty tip

Any vegetables work well with this omelet. Try sliced scallions, fine strips of red or green bell peppers, snow peas halved lengthwise, or a few green beans. Cut them into even-size pieces so that they are all tender at the same time.

Mediterranean Feast

1 Quarter the lettuce and remove the hard core. Tear into bite-size pieces and arrange on a large serving platter or four individual plates.

2 Cook the green beans in boiling, salted water for 8 minutes, and the potatoes for 10 minutes or until tender. Drain and rinse in cold water until cool, then cut both the beans and potatoes in half with a sharp knife.

3 Boil the eggs for 10 minutes, then rinse thoroughly under cold running water until cool. Remove the shells under the water, then cut each egg into four.

4 Remove the seeds from the bell pepper and cut into thin strips. Finely chop the onion.

5 Arrange the beans, potatoes, eggs, bell peppers, and onion on top of the lettuce. Add the tuna, cheese, and tomatoes. Sprinkle with the olives and garnish with the basil.

6 To make the vinaigrette, place all the ingredients in a screw-top jar, and shake vigorously until everything is mixed thoroughly. Spoon 4 tablespoons over the top of the prepared salad, and serve the remainder separately.

Ingredients   SERVES 4

1 small head of lettuce
1¹/₂ cups fine green beans
8 oz. baby new potatoes, scrubbed
4 large eggs
1 green bell pepper
1 medium onion, peeled
7oz. canned tuna in water, drained
   and flaked into small pieces
¹/₂ cup diced reduced-fat hard
   cheese, such as cheddar
8 ripe but firm cherry
   tomatoes, quartered
5 tbsp. pitted ripe olives, halved
freshly chopped basil, to garnish

For the lime vinaigrette:

3 tbsp. light olive oil
2 tbsp. white wine vinegar
4 tbsp. lime juice
2 tsp. grated lime rind
1 tsp. mustard
1-2 tsp. sugar
salt and freshly ground
   black pepper

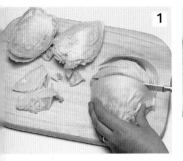

Mozzarella Frittata with Tomato & Basil Salad

1 To make the tomato and basil salad, slice the tomatoes very thinly, tear the basil leaves, and sprinkle the basil over the tomatoes. Make the dressing by beating the olive oil, lemon juice, and sugar together. Season with pepper before drizzling the dressing over the salad.

2 To make the frittata, place the eggs in a large bowl with plenty of salt and beat. Shred the mozzarella and stir into the egg with the finely chopped scallions.

3 Heat the oil in a nonstick skillet and pour in the egg mixture, stirring with a wooden spoon to spread the ingredients evenly over the skillet.

4 Cook for 5–8 minutes until the frittata is golden brown and firm on the underside. Place the whole skillet under the broiler, and cook for about 4–5 minutes until the top is golden brown. Slide the frittata onto a serving plate, cut into six large wedges, and serve immediately with the tomato and basil salad and plenty of warm, crusty bread.

Ingredients
SERVES 6

For the salad:
6 ripe but firm tomatoes
2 tbsp. fresh basil leaves
2 tbsp. olive oil
1 tbsp. fresh lemon juice
1 tsp. sugar
freshly ground black pepper

For the frittata:
7 large eggs, beaten
salt
$2^3/_4$ cups mozzarella cheese
2 scallions, trimmed and
    finely chopped
2 tbsp. olive oil
warm, crusty bread, to serve

Helpful hint
Fresh mozzarella is sold in packages and is sometimes surrounded by a light brine. After shredding the cheese, firmly press between layers of paper towels to remove any excess water that might leak out during cooking.

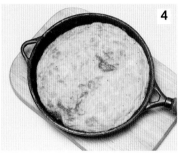

Tomato & Zucchini Herb Tart

1 Preheat the oven to 450°F. Heat 2 tablespoons of the oil in a large skillet.

2 Fry the onion and garlic for about 4 minutes until softened, and set aside.

3 Roll out the pastry on a lightly floured surface, and cut out a 12-inch circle.

4 Brush the pastry with a little beaten egg, then prick all over with a fork.

5 Transfer onto a dampened baking sheet and bake in the preheated oven for about 10 minutes.

6 Turn the pastry over and brush with a little more egg. Bake for 5 more minutes, then remove from the oven.

7 Mix together the onion, garlic, and herbs with the goat cheese, and spread over the pastry. Arrange the tomatoes and zucchini over the goat cheese, and drizzle with the remaining oil.

8 Cook for 20–25 minutes until the pastry is golden brown and the topping is bubbling. Garnish with the thyme sprigs and serve immediately.

Ingredients   SERVES 4

4 tbsp. olive oil
1 onion, peeled and finely chopped
3 garlic cloves, peeled and crushed
14 oz. prepared puff pastry, thawed
   if frozen
1 small egg, beaten
2 tbsp. freshly chopped rosemary
2 tbsp. freshly chopped parsley
6 oz. rindless, fresh, soft goat cheese
4 ripe plum tomatoes, sliced
1 medium zucchini, trimmed
   and sliced
thyme sprigs, to garnish

Food fact

Goat cheese works particularly well in this recipe, complementing both the tomatoes and zucchini. Be aware, though, that it can be a little acidic, so try to choose a creamy variety, which will mellow even more when baked.

Sicilian Baked Eggplant

1   Preheat the oven to 400°F. Cut the eggplant into small cubes and place on a greased baking sheet. Cover the baking sheet with foil and cook in the preheated oven for about 15–20 minutes until soft. Set aside to let the eggplant cool.

2   Place the celery and tomatoes in a large bowl, and cover with boiling water.

3   Remove the tomatoes from the bowl when their skins begin to peel away. Remove the skins, then seed and chop the flesh into small pieces.

4   Remove the celery from the bowl of water, finely chop, and set aside.

5   Pour the vegetable oil into a nonstick saucepan, add the chopped shallots, and cook gently for 2–3 minutes until soft. Add the celery, tomatoes, tomato paste, and olives. Season to taste with salt and pepper.

6   Simmer gently for 3–4 minutes. Add the vinegar, sugar, and cooled eggplant to the saucepan and heat gently for 2–3 minutes until all the ingredients are well blended. Set aside to let the eggplant mixture cool. When cool, garnish with the chopped basil and serve with lettuce leaves.

Ingredients   SERVES 4

1 large eggplant, trimmed
2 celery stalks, trimmed
4 large ripe tomatoes
1 tsp. corn oil
2 shallots, peeled and finely chopped
1½ tsp. tomato paste
2 tbsp. pitted green olives
2 tbsp. pitted ripe olives
salt and freshly ground
    black pepper
1 tbsp. white wine vinegar
2 tsp. sugar
1 tbsp. freshly chopped basil,
    to garnish
mixed lettuce leaves, to serve

Food fact

It has been suggested that foods that are purple in color, such as eggplants, have particularly powerful antioxidants, which help the body protect itself from disease and strengthen the organs.

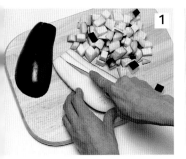
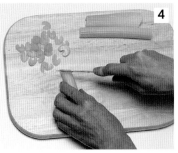

Corn Fritters with Hot & Spicy Relish

1   Make the relish. Heat a wok, add the sunflower oil, and, when hot, add the onion and stir-fry for 3–4 minutes until softened. Add the chiles, and garlic, stir-fry for 1 minute, then let cool slightly. Stir in the plum sauce, transfer to a food processor, and blend until the consistency of chutney. Set aside.

2   Place the corn kernels in a food processor and blend briefly until just mashed. Transfer to a bowl with the onions, chili powder, coriander, flour, baking powder, and egg. Season to taste with salt and pepper, and mix together.

3   Heat a wok, add the oil, and heat to 350°F. Working in batches, drop a few spoonfuls of the corn mixture into the oil, and deep-fry for 3–4 minutes until golden and crispy, turning occasionally. Using a slotted spoon, remove and drain on paper towels. Arrange on a warmed serving platter, garnish with sprigs of cilantro, and serve immediately with the relish.

Ingredients   MAKES 16–20

11oz. canned corn kernels, drained
1 onion, peeled and very
   finely chopped
1 scallion, trimmed and very
   finely chopped
$1/2$ tsp. chili powder
1 tsp. ground coriander
4 tbsp. all-purpose flour
1 tsp. baking powder
1 large egg
salt and freshly ground black pepper
$1^1/_4$ cups peanut oil
cilantro,sprigs to garnish

For the spicy relish:

3 tbsp. sunflower oil
1 onion, peeled and very
   finely chopped
$1/4$ tsp. dried, crushed chiles
2 garlic cloves, peeled and crushed
2 tbsp. plum sauce

Creamy Lentils

1 Put the lentils in a saucepan with plenty of cold water, and bring to a boil.

2 Boil rapidly for 10 minutes, reduce the heat, and simmer gently for an additional 20 minutes until tender. Drain well.

3 Meanwhile, prepare the dressing. Heat the oil in a skillet over a medium heat.

4 Add the garlic and cook for about a minute until just beginning to brown. Add the lemon zest and juice.

5 Add the mustard and cook for an additional 30 seconds.

6 Add the tarragon and sour cream, and season to taste with salt and pepper.

7 Simmer and add the drained lentils, tomatoes, and olives.

8 Transfer to a serving dish and sprinkle the chopped parsley on top. Garnish the lentils with the tarragon sprigs and the lemon wedges, and serve immediately.

Ingredients   SERVES 4

$1\frac{1}{4}$ cups lentils
1 tbsp. olive oil
1 garlic clove, peeled and finely chopped
1 tbsp. lemon zest
2 tbsp. lemon juice
1 tsp. mustard
1 tbsp. freshly chopped tarragon
3 tbsp. reduced-fat sour cream
salt and freshly ground black pepper
2 small tomatoes, seeded and chopped
5 tbsp. pitted ripe olives
1 tbsp. freshly chopped parsley

To garnish:
fresh tarragon sprigs
lemon wedges

Food fact
Puy lentils are smaller and fatter than green lentils, and have a mottled coloring, ranging from gold to green. They keep their shape and firm texture when cooked. They may not always be French, however, as this type of lentil is also grown extensively in Canada.

Bean & Cashew Stir-Fry

1 Heat a wok or large skillet, add the oil, and, when hot, add the onion and celery, and stir-fry gently for 3–4 minutes until softened.

2 Add the ginger, garlic, and chile to the wok, and stir-fry for 30 seconds. Stir in the green beans, snow peas, and cashews, and continue to stir-fry for 1–2 minutes until the nuts are golden brown.

3 Dissolve the sugar in the stock, then blend with the sherry, soy sauce, and vinegar. Stir into the bean mixture, and bring to a boil. Simmer gently, stirring occasionally, for 3–4 minutes until the beans and snow peas are tender but still crisp, and the sauce has thickened slightly. Season to taste with salt and pepper. Transfer to a warmed serving bowl, or spoon onto individual plates. Sprinkle with freshly chopped cilantro and serve immediately.

Ingredients SERVES 4

3 tbsp. sunflower oil
1 onion, peeled and finely chopped
1 celery stalk, trimmed and chopped
1-in. piece ginger, peeled and grated
2 garlic cloves, peeled and crushed
1 red chile, deseeded and
 finely chopped
1 cup trimmed and halved fine
 green beans
$1^1/_4$ cups diagonally sliced
 snow-pea thirds
$2^1/_3$ cups unsalted cashews
1 tsp. brown sugar
$^1/_2$ cup vegetable stock
2 tbsp. dry sherry
1 tbsp. light soy sauce
1 tsp. red wine vinegar
salt and freshly ground black pepper
freshly chopped cilantro, to garnish

Chicken & Baby Vegetable Stir-Fry

1   Heat the wok until very hot and add the oil. Add the chopped chile and chicken, and stir-fry for 4–5 minutes until the chicken is cooked and golden.

2   Increase the heat, add the leeks to the chicken, and stir-fry for 2 minutes. Add the asparagus spears, snow peas, baby carrots, green beans, and baby corn. Stir-fry for 3–4 minutes until the vegetables soften slightly but still retain a slight crispness.

3   In a small bowl, mix together the chicken stock, soy sauce, dry sherry, and sesame oil. Pour into the wok, stir, and cook until heated through. Sprinkle with the toasted sesame seeds and serve immediately.

Ingredients   SERVES 4

2 tbsp. peanut oil

1 small red chile, seeded and finely chopped

$^1/_3$ lb. chicken breast or thigh meat, skinned and cut into cubes

2 baby leeks, trimmed and sliced

12 asparagus spears, halved

1 cup trimmed snow peas

1 cup trimmed and halved baby carrots

$^3/_4$ cup trimmed and diagonally sliced fine green beans

1 cup diagonally halved baby corn

$^1/_4$ cup chicken stock

2 tsp. light soy sauce

1 tbsp. dry sherry

1 tsp. sesame oil

toasted sesame seeds, to garnish

Helpful hint

Look for packages of mixed baby vegetables in the supermarket. They are often available ready to eat, which will save a lot of time.

Chicken Satay Salad

1 Place the peanut butter, chili sauce, garlic, vinegar, soy sauces, sugar, salt, and ground peppercorns in a food processor and blend to form a smooth paste. Scrape into a bowl, cover with plastic wrap, and chill in the refrigerator until required.

2 Bring a large saucepan of lightly salted water to a boil. Add the noodles and cook for 3–5 minutes. Drain, then plunge into cold water. Drain again and toss in the sesame oil. Let cool.

3 Heat the wok until very hot, add the oil, and, when hot, add the chicken cubes. Stir-fry for 5–6 minutes until the chicken is golden brown and cooked through.

4 Remove the chicken from the wok using a slotted spoon and add to the noodles, along with the peanut sauce. Mix lightly together, then sprinkle with the shredded celery leaves, and either serve immediately or leave until cold, then serve with romaine lettuce.

Ingredients   SERVES 4

4 tbsp. crunchy peanut butter

1 tbsp. chili sauce

1 garlic clove, peeled and crushed

2 tbsp. vinegar

2 tbsp. light soy sauce

2 tbsp. dark soy sauce

2 tsp. brown sugar

pinch salt

2 tsp. freshly ground Sichuan or black peppercorns

$6^2/_3$ cups dried egg noodles

2 tbsp. sesame oil

1 tbsp. peanut oil

1 lb. skinless, boneless chicken breast fillets, cut into cubes

shredded celery leaves, to garnish

romaine lettuce, to serve

Food fact

Sichuan peppercorns are the dried berries of a shrub which is a member of the citrus family. They have a sharp, mildly spicy flavor. They are often toasted in a dry skillet before grinding to bring out their distinctive flavor.

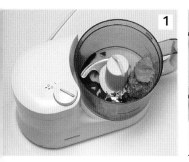

Crispy Baked Potatoes with Prosciutto

1 Preheat the oven to 400°F. Scrub the potatoes dry. Prick with a fork and place on a baking sheet. Cook for 1–1½ hours until tender when squeezed. Use oven mitts to pick up the potatoes, as they will be very hot.

2 Cut the potatoes in half horizontally and scoop out all the flesh into a bowl.

3 Spoon the sour cream into the bowl and mix thoroughly with the potatoes. Season to taste with a little salt and pepper.

4 Cut the ham or prosciutto into fine strips, and carefully stir into the potato mixture with the fava beans, carrots, and peas.

5 Pile the mixture back into the 8 potato shells and sprinkle a little shredded cheese over the top.

6 Place under a hot broiler and cook until golden and heated through. Serve immediately with a fresh green salad.

Ingredients   SERVES 4

4 large baking potatoes
4 tsp. reduced-fat sour cream
salt and freshly ground
    black pepper
2 slices lean serrano ham or
    prosciutto
1 cup cooked baby fava beans
¼ cup diced cooked carrots
1 cup cooked peas
½ cup shredded reduced-fat hard
    cheese such as cheddar
fresh green salad, to serve

Food fact

Produced in Spain, serrano ham has a succulent, sweet taste and is traditionally carved along the grain. The nearest substitute is prosciutto. Serrano ham has a chewy texture and is often served in thin slices on bread.

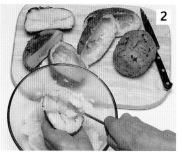

Beef Fajitas with Avocado Sauce

1 Heat the wok, add the oil, then stir-fry the beef for 3–4 minutes. Add the garlic and spices, and cook for an additional 2 minutes. Stir the tomatoes into the wok, bring to a boil, cover, and simmer gently for 5 minutes.

2 Meanwhile, blend the kidney beans in a food processor until slightly broken up, then add to the wok. Continue to cook for an additional 5 minutes, adding 2–3 tablespoons of water. The mixture should be thick and fairly dry. Stir in the chopped cilantro.

3 Mix the chopped avocado, shallot, tomato, chile, and lemon juice together. Spoon into a serving dish and set aside.

4 When ready to serve, warm the flour tortillas and spread with a little sour cream. Place a spoonful of the beef mixture on top, followed by a spoonful of the avocado sauce, then roll up. Repeat until all the mixture is used up. Serve immediately with a green salad.

Ingredients   SERVES 3–6

2 tbsp. corn oil

1-lb. rump steak, trimmed and cut into strips

2 garlic cloves, peeled and crushed

1 tsp. ground cumin

$1/4$ tsp. cayenne pepper

1 tbsp. paprika

8oz. canned chopped tomatoes

7oz. canned red kidney beans, drained

1 tbsp. freshly chopped cilantro

1 avocado, peeled, pitted, and chopped

1 shallot, peeled and chopped

1 large tomato, peeled, seeded, and chopped

1 red chile, diced

1 tbsp. lemon juice

6 large flour tortillas

3–4 tbsp. sour cream

green salad, to serve

Rice & Pasta

Rice and pasta are suitable for any occasion and are cheap, filling, and delicious—what more could one ask of a meal? Rice and fish are a particularly good combo: try Smoked Haddock Kedgeree or Pan-Fried Salmon with Herb Risotto. Pasta lends itself to flavorsome, bold sauces, so what could be more tasty than Rigatoni with Gorgonzola & Walnuts or Creamed Lamb & Wild Mushroom Pasta?

Rice-Filled Peppers

1   Preheat the oven to 400°F. Put the tomatoes in a small bowl, and add boiling water to cover. Leave for 1 minute, then drain. Plunge the tomatoes into cold water to cool, then peel off the skins. Quarter, remove the seeds, and chop.

2   Heat the olive oil in a skillet, and cook the onion gently for 10 minutes until softened. Add the garlic, chopped tomatoes, and sugar.

3   Gently cook the tomato mixture for 10 minutes until thickened. Remove from the heat and stir the rice, pine nuts, and oregano into the sauce. Season to taste with salt and pepper.

4   Halve the bell peppers lengthwise, cutting through and leaving the stem on. Remove the seeds and cores, then put the bell peppers in a lightly greased roasting pan, cut-side down, and cook in the preheated oven for 10 minutes.

5   Turn the bell peppers so they are cut-side up. Spoon in the filling, then cover with foil. Return to the oven for 15 minutes or until the bell peppers are very tender, removing the foil for the last 5 minutes to allow the tops to brown a little.

6   Serve 1 red and 1 yellow bell pepper half to each person, along with a mixed salad and crusty bread.

Ingredients   SERVES 4

8 ripe tomatoes
2 tbsp. olive oil
1 onion, peeled and chopped
1 garlic clove, peeled and crushed
$\frac{1}{2}$ tsp. dark brown sugar
$1\frac{1}{2}$ cups cooked long-grain rice
$\frac{1}{2}$ cup toasted pine nuts
1 tbsp. freshly chopped oregano
salt and freshly ground black pepper
2 large red bell peppers
2 large yellow bell peppers

To serve:

mixed salad
crusty bread

Helpful hint

It may be necessary to take a very thin slice from the bottom of the bell peppers to enable them to stand on the baking sheet. Be careful not to cut right through.

Aduki Bean & Rice Burgers

1 Heat 1 tablespoon of the oil in a saucepan and gently cook the onion for 10 minutes until soft. Add the garlic and curry paste, and cook for a few more seconds. Stir in the rice and beans.

2 Pour in the stock, bring to a boil, and simmer for 12 minutes or until all the stock has been absorbed—do not lift the lid for the first 10 minutes of cooking. Set aside.

3 Lightly mash the tofu. Add to the rice mixture with the garam masala, cilantro, salt, and pepper. Mix. Shape the mixture in eight patties. Chill in the refrigerator for 30 minutes.

4 Meanwhile, make the raita. Mix together the carrots, cucumber, and plain yogurt. Spoon into a small bowl and chill in the refrigerator until ready to serve.

5 Heat the remaining oil in a large skillet. Fry the patties, in batches if necessary, for 4–5 minutes on each side until lightly browned. Serve in the buns with tomato slices and lettuce. Accompany with the raita.

Ingredients　　　SERVES 4

2$\frac{1}{2}$ tbsp. sunflower oil

1 medium onion, peeled and very finely chopped

1 garlic clove, peeled and crushed

1 tsp. curry paste

1$\frac{1}{3}$ cups basmati rice

14oz. canned aduki beans, drained and rinsed (kidney beans may also be used)

1 cup vegetable stock

$\frac{1}{4}$ lb. firm tofu, crumbled

1 tsp. garam masala

2 tbsp. freshly chopped cilantro

salt and freshly ground black pepper

For the carrot raita:

2 large carrots, peeled and shredded

$\frac{1}{2}$ cucumber, diced

$\frac{2}{3}$ cup plain yogurt

To serve:

whole-wheat hamburger buns

tomato slices

lettuce leaves

Fried Rice with Bamboo Shoots & Ginger

1 Heat a wok, add the oil, and, when hot, add the onion and cook gently for 3–4 minutes. Add the rice and cook for 3–4 minutes until golden, stirring frequently.

2 Add the garlic, ginger, and chopped scallions to the wok, and stir well. Pour the chicken stock into a small saucepan and bring to a boil. Carefully ladle the hot stock into the wok, stir well, then simmer gently for 10 minutes or until most of the liquid has been absorbed.

3 Stir the button mushrooms, peas, and soy sauce into the wok, and continue to cook for an additional 5 minutes or until the rice is tender, adding a little extra stock if necessary.

4 Add the bamboo shoots to the wok and carefully stir in. Season to taste with salt, pepper, and cayenne pepper. Cook for 2–3 minutes until heated through. Tip onto a warmed serving dish, garnish with cilantro, and serve immediately.

Ingredients SERVES 4

4 tbsp. sunflower oil

1 onion, peeled and finely chopped

$1^1/_3$ cups long-grain rice

3 garlic cloves, peeled and cut into slivers

1-in. piece ginger, peeled and grated

3 scallions, trimmed and chopped

2 cups vegetable stock

$^1/_4$ lb. button mushrooms, wiped and halved

$^1/_2$ cup thawed frozen peas

2 tbsp. light soy sauce

17oz. canned bamboo shoots, drained and thinly sliced

salt and freshly ground black pepper

cayenne pepper, to taste

fresh cilantro, to garnish

Food fact

Button, cap and flat mushrooms are actually the same type of mushroom but in different stages of maturity. The button mushroom is the youngest and therefore has the mildest flavor.

Smoked Haddock Kedgeree

1 Place the haddock in a shallow skillet, and cover with 1¼ cups water. Simmer gently for 8–10 minutes until the fish is cooked. Drain, then remove all the skin and bones from the fish, and flake into a dish. Keep warm.

2 Melt the butter in a saucepan and add the chopped onion and curry powder. Cook, stirring, for 3–4 minutes until the onion is soft, then stir in the rice. Cook for an additional minute, stirring continuously, then stir in the hot stock.

3 Cover and simmer gently for 15 minutes or until the rice has absorbed all the liquid. Cut the eggs into quarters or eighths, and add half to the mixture with half the parsley.

4 Carefully fold the cooked fish into the mixture and add the cream, if desired. Season to taste with salt and pepper. Heat the kedgeree until piping hot.

5 Transfer the mixture to a large dish, garnish with the remaining quartered eggs and parsley, and season with a pinch of cayenne pepper. Serve immediately.

Ingredients SERVES 4

1 lb. smoked haddock fillet
4 tbsp. butter
1 onion, peeled and finely chopped
2 tsp. mild curry powder
1 cup long-grain rice
2 cups fish or vegetable
   stock, heated
2 extra-large eggs, hard-boiled
   and peeled
2 tbsp. freshly chopped parsley
2 tbsp. whipping cream (optional)
salt and freshly ground black pepper
pinch cayenne pepper

Food fact

The word *khichri* means a "mixture," in Hindi. The British in India adapted this dish of lentils, rice and spices into kedgeree by adding smoked fish and hard-boiled eggs. If smoked haddock is unavailable, use smoked salmon instead.

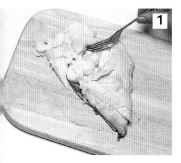

Spicy Cod Rice

1 Mix together the flour, cilantro, cumin, and ground coriander on a large plate. Coat the cod in the spice mixture, then place on a baking tray, cover, and chill in the refrigerator for 30 minutes.

2 Heat a large wok, then add 2 tablespoons of the oil and heat until almost smoking. Stir-fry the cashews for 1 minute until brown, then remove and set aside.

3 Add an additional tablespoon of the oil and heat until almost smoking. Add the cod and stir-fry for 2 minutes. Using a spatula, turn the cod pieces over and cook for an additional 2 minutes until golden. Transfer to a warm plate, cover, and keep warm.

4 Add the remaining oil to the wok, heat until almost smoking, then stir-fry the scallions and chile for 1 minute before adding the carrots and peas, and stir-frying for an additional 2 minutes. Stir in the rice, chili sauce, soy sauce, and cashews, and stir-fry for 3 more minutes. Add the cod, heat for 1 minute, then serve immediately.

Ingredients   SERVES 4

1 tbsp. all-purpose flour
1 tbsp. freshly chopped cilantro
1 tsp. ground cumin
1 tsp. ground coriander
$1^{1}/_{4}$-lb. thick-cut cod fillet, skinned and
    cut into large chunks
4 tbsp. peanut oil
$^{1}/_{2}$ cup cashews
1 bunch scallions, trimmed and
    diagonally sliced
1 red chile, seeded and chopped
1 carrot, peeled and cut into matchsticks
1 cup frozen peas
5 cups cooked long-grain rice
2 tbsp. sweet chili sauce
2 tbsp. soy sauce

Helpful hint

Care is needed when frying nuts, as they have a tendency to burn very quickly. An alternative is to toast them on a baking tray in the oven at 350°F for about 5 minutes until they are golden and fragrant.

Pan-Fried Salmon with Herb Risotto

1   Wipe the salmon fillets with a clean, damp cloth. Mix together the flour, mustard powder, and seasoning on a large plate, and use to coat the salmon fillets. Set aside.

2   Heat half the olive oil in a large skillet, and cook the shallots for 5 minutes until softened but not browned. Add the rice and stir for 1 minute, then slowly add the wine, bring to a boil and boil rapidly until reduced by half.

3   Bring the stock to a gentle simmer, then add to the rice, a ladleful at a time. Cook, stirring frequently, adding the stock as needed until the rice is cooked yet firm. Stir in the butter, freshly chopped herbs, and season to taste with salt and pepper.

4   Heat the remaining olive oil and the pat of butter in a large griddle pan, add the salmon fillets, and cook for 2–3 minutes on each side until done. Arrange the herb risotto on warm serving plates and top with the salmon. Garnish with slices of lemon and sprigs of dill, and serve immediately with a tomato salad.

Ingredients   SERVES 4

4 salmon fillets
3–4 tbsp. all-purpose flour
1 tsp. dried mustard powder
salt and freshly ground black pepper
2 tbsp. olive oil
3 shallots, peeled and chopped
1 cup risotto rice
$^2/_3$ cup dry white wine
$5^1/_4$ cups vegetable or fish stock
4 tbsp. butter
2 tbsp. freshly cut chives
2 tbsp. freshly chopped dill
2 tbsp. freshly chopped Italian parsley
pat of butter

To garnish:

lemon slices
fresh dill sprigs
tomato salad, to serve

Helpful hint

Stirring the butter into the risotto at the end is an important step, giving the dish its fine texture and a beautiful shine. Serve risotto as soon as it is cooked.

Thai Fried Rice with Shrimp & Chiles

1 Wash the rice in several changes of water until the water remains relatively clear. Drain well. Bring a large saucepan of salted water to a boil and add the rice. Cook for 12–15 minutes until tender. Drain well and set aside.

2 Heat a wok, add the oil, and, when very hot, add the garlic and stir-fry for 20 seconds or until just browned. Add the chiles and shrimp, and stir-fry for 2–3 minutes.

3 Add the fish sauce, sugar, and soy sauce, and stir-fry for another 30 seconds or until the shrimp are cooked through.

4 Add the cooked rice to the wok and stir together well. Add the onion, red bell pepper, and scallion, mix together for an additional minute, then turn onto a serving platter. Garnish with sprigs of fresh cilantro and serve immediately.

Ingredients   SERVES 4

1 cup Thai fragrant rice
2 tbsp. peanut or vegetable oil
2 garlic cloves, peeled and
   finely chopped
2 red chiles, seeded and
   finely chopped
1 cup shelled raw shrimp
1 tbsp. Thai fish sauce
$^1/_4$ tsp. sugar
1 tbsp. light soy sauce
$^1/_2$ small onion, peeled and finely sliced
$^1/_2$ red bell pepper, seeded and
   finely sliced
1 scallion, green part only, cut into
   long strips
fresh cilantro sprigs, to garnish

Food fact

Thai fragrant rice is a good-quality long-grain rice with a delicate scent. The rice should be washed in several changes of water, until the water remains relatively clear, and then drained. Cook the rice according to the directions on the packet.

Persian Chicken Pilaf

1 Heat the oil in a large, heavy saucepan over a medium-high heat. Cook the chicken pieces in batches until lightly browned. Return all the browned chicken to the saucepan.

2 Add the onions to the saucepan, reduce the heat to medium, and cook for 3–5 minutes, stirring frequently, until the onions begin to soften. Add the cumin and rice, and stir to coat the rice. Cook for about 2 minutes until the rice is golden and translucent. Stir in the tomato paste and the saffron strands, then season to taste with salt and pepper.

3 Add the pomegranate juice and stock, and bring to a boil, stirring once or twice. Add the apricots and raisins, and stir gently. Reduce the heat to low and cook for 30 minutes until the chicken and rice are tender and the liquid is absorbed.

4 Turn into a shallow serving dish and sprinkle with the chopped mint or parsley. Serve immediately, garnished with pomegranate seeds, if desired.

Ingredients   SERVES 4–6

2–3 tbsp. vegetable oil
1¹/₂ lbs. boneless, skinless chicken pieces
    (breast and thighs), cut into
    1-in. pieces
2 medium onions, peeled and
    coarsely chopped
1 tsp. ground cumin
heaping 1 cup long-grain white rice
1 tbsp. tomato paste
1 tsp. saffron strands
salt and freshly ground black pepper
1 cup pomegranate juice
3³/₄ cups chicken stock
1 cup halved and pitted dried apricots
    or prunes
2 tbsp. raisins
2 tbsp. freshly chopped mint or parsley
pomegranate seeds,
    to garnish (optional)

Helpful hint

Substitute unsweetened grape
or apple juice if you cannot get
pomegranate juice.

Italian Risotto

1. Chop the onion and garlic, and set aside. Heat the olive oil in a large skillet, and cook the salami for 3–5 minutes until golden. Transfer to a plate and keep warm. Add the asparagus and stir-fry for 2–3 minutes until just wilted. Transfer to the plate with the salami. Add the onion and garlic, and cook for 5 minutes or until softened.

2. Add the rice to the skillet and cook for 2 minutes. Add the wine, bring to a boil, then simmer, stirring until the wine has been absorbed. Add half the stock and return to a boil. Simmer, stirring, until the liquid has been absorbed.

3. Add half of the remaining stock and the fava beans to the rice mixture. Bring to a boil, then simmer for an additional 5–10 minutes until all of the liquid has been absorbed.

4. Add the remaining stock, bring to a boil, then simmer until all the liquid is absorbed and the rice is tender. Stir in the remaining ingredients until the cheese has just melted. Serve immediately.

Ingredients   SERVES 4

1 onion, peeled
2 garlic cloves, peeled
1 tbsp. olive oil
2 cups chopped Italian salami
$^1/_2$ cup asparagus tips
$1^1/_2$ cups risotto rice
$1^1/_4$ cups dry white wine
4 cups chicken stock, warmed
$^3/_4$ cup thawed frozen fava beans
1 cup diced dolcelatte or blue cheese
3 tbsp. freshly chopped mixed herbs, such as parsley and basil
salt and freshly ground black pepper

Food fact

Cheese is a common ingredient in the making of risotto and in fact helps to provide some of its creamy texture. Usually Parmesan cheese is added at the end of cooking, but here a good-quality dolcelatte or blue cheese is used instead.

Antipasto Penne

1 Preheat the broiler just before cooking. Cut the zucchini into thick slices. Cut the tomatoes into quarters, then cut the ham into strips. Pour the oil into a baking dish, and place under the broiler for 2 minutes or until almost smoking. Remove from the broiler and stir in the zucchini. Return to the broiler and cook for 8 minutes. Remove from the broiler and add the tomatoes and cook for 3 minutes.

2 Add the ham to the baking dish and cook under the broiler for 4 minutes until all the vegetables are charred and the ham is brown. Season to taste with salt and pepper.

3 Meanwhile, plunge the pasta into a large saucepan of lightly salted, boiling water, return to a rolling boil, stir, and cook for 8 minutes or until tender but still firm to the bite. Drain well and return to the saucepan.

4 Stir the antipasto into the vegetables and cook under the broiler for 2 minutes or until heated through. Add the cooked pasta and toss together gently with the remaining ingredients. Broil for an additional 4 minutes, then serve immediately.

Ingredients
SERVES 4

3 medium zucchini, trimmed
4 tomatoes
$1\frac{1}{2}$ cups Italian ham
2 tbsp. olive oil
salt and freshly ground black pepper
$4\frac{1}{2}$ cups dried penne pasta
10 oz. canned antipasto
1 cup drained and diced
　mozzarella cheese
1 cup crumbled Gorgonzola cheese
3 tbsp. freshly chopped Italian
　flat-leaf parsley

Food fact

The term "antipasto" refers to the course served before the pasto, or "meal," begins. Its purpose is to whet the appetite for the following courses. In Italy, these are served in small quantities, though two or three different dishes may be served at once. There are no rigid rules as to what constitutes a suitable dish for antipasti—there are thousands of regional variations.

Rigatoni with Gorgonzola & Walnuts

1 Bring a large pan of lightly salted water to a rolling boil. Add the rigatoni and cook according to the package directions until tender but still firm to the bite. Drain the pasta thoroughly, then set aside and keep warm.

2 Melt the butter in a large pan or wok over a medium heat. Add the Gorgonzola cheese and stir until just melted. Add the brandy (if desired) and cook for 30 seconds, then pour in the whipping or heavy cream and cook for 1–2 minutes, stirring until the sauce is smooth.

3 Stir in the walnut pieces, basil, and half the Parmesan cheese, then add the rigatoni. Season with salt and pepper. Return to the heat, stirring frequently, until heated through. Divide the pasta among four warmed bowls, then sprinkle with the remaining Parmesan cheese and serve immediately with cherry tomatoes and fresh green.

Ingredients
SERVES 4

$3^1/_2$ cups rigatoni
4 tbsp. butter
1 cup crumbled Gorgonzola cheese
2 tbsp. brandy, optional
$^3/_4$ cup whipping or heavy cream
$^1/_2$ cup lightly toasted and coarsely chopped walnut pieces
1 tbsp. freshly chopped basil
$^1/_2$ cup freshly grated Parmesan cheese
salt and freshly ground black pepper

To serve:
cherry tomatoes
fresh green

Tasty tip
This blue cheese sauce is also very good with pappardelle or lasagnette, both very wide egg pasta noodles. If preferred, you could use sour cream, but it must be heated gently as it can curdle at high temperatures.

Gnocchetti with Broccoli & Bacon Sauce

1 Bring a large pan of salted water to a boil. Add the broccoli florets and cook for about 8–10 minutes until very soft. Drain thoroughly and leave to cool slightly; then chop finely and set aside.

2 Heat the olive oil in a heavy pan. Add the pancetta or bacon and cook over a medium heat for 5 minutes or until golden and crisp. Add the onion and cook for an additional 5 minutes or until soft and lightly golden. Add the garlic and cook for 1 minute.

3 Transfer the chopped broccoli to the bacon or pancetta mixture and pour in the milk. Bring slowly to a boil and simmer rapidly for about 15 minutes until reduced to a creamy texture.

4 Meanwhile, bring a large pan of lightly salted water to a rolling boil. Add the pasta and cook according to the package directions until tender but still firm to the bite.

5 Drain the pasta thoroughly, setting aside a little of the cooking water. Add the pasta and the Parmesan cheese to the broccoli mixture. Toss, adding enough of the cooking water to make a creamy sauce. Season to taste with salt and pepper. Serve immediately with extra Parmesan cheese.

Ingredients   SERVES 6

1 lb. broccoli florets

4 tbsp. olive oil

$1/2$ cup finely chopped pancetta or smoked bacon

1 small onion, peeled and finely chopped

3 garlic cloves, peeled and sliced

$3/4$ cup milk

4 cups gnocchetti (little elongated ribbed shells)

$1/2$ cup freshly grated Parmesan cheese, plus extra to serve

salt and freshly ground black pepper

Food fact

Pancetta is an Italian bacon that may be either smoked or unsmoked. You can buy it sliced or in a piece, but it is often sold prepacked, cut into tiny cubes ready for cooking. Thickly cut, smoked bacon makes a good alternative.

Gnocchi & Prosciutto Bake

1 Heat the oven to 350°F. Heat 2 tablespoons of the olive oil in a large skillet and cook the onion and garlic for 5 minutes or until softened. Stir in the tomatoes, sun-dried tomato paste, and mascarpone cheese. Season to taste with salt and pepper. Add half the tarragon. Bring to a boil, then lower the heat immediately and simmer for 5 minutes.

2 Meanwhile, bring 8 cups water to a boil in a large pan. Add the remaining olive oil and a good pinch of salt. Add the gnocchi and cook for 1–2 minutes until they rise to the surface.

3 Drain the gnocchi thoroughly and transfer to a large ovenproof dish. Add the tomato sauce and toss gently to coat the pasta. Combine the cheddar or Parmesan cheese with the bread crumbs and remaining tarragon and spread over the pasta mixture. Top with the prosciutto and olives and season again.

4 Cook in the preheated oven for 20–25 minutes until golden and bubbling. Serve immediately, garnished with parsley sprigs.

Ingredients   SERVES 4

3 tbsp. olive oil
1 red onion, peeled and sliced
2 garlic cloves, peeled
3 plum tomatoes, skinned
    and quartered
2 tbsp. sun-dried tomato paste
1 cup mascarpone cheese
salt and freshly ground black pepper
1 tbsp. freshly chopped tarragon
11 oz. fresh gnocchi
1 cup grated cheddar or Parmesan
1 cup fresh white bread crumbs
2 oz. prosciutto, sliced
10 pitted green olives, halved
Italian flat-leaf parsley sprigs,
    to garnish

Helpful hint

Make sure that you buy gnocchi potato dumplings for this recipe and not gnocchi sardi, a pasta of the same name. It is important to use a large pan of boiling water so that they have plenty of room to move around, otherwise they will stick together.

Chorizo with Pasta in a Tomato Sauce

1 Melt the butter with the olive oil in a large heavy pan. Add the onions and sugar, and cook over a very low heat, stirring occasionally, for 15 minutes or until soft and starting to caramelize.

2 Add the garlic and chorizo to the pan and cook for 5 minutes. Stir in the chile, chopped tomatoes, and tomato paste, and pour in the wine. Season well with salt and pepper. Bring to a boil, cover, reduce the heat, and simmer for 30 minutes, stirring occasionally. Remove the lid and simmer for an additional 10 minutes or until the sauce starts to thicken.

3 Meanwhile, bring a large pan of lightly salted water to a rolling boil. Add the pasta and cook according to the package directions until tender but still firm to the bite.

4 Drain the pasta, setting aside 2 tablespoons of the water, and return to the pan. Add the chorizo sauce with the cooking water, and toss gently until the pasta is evenly covered. Spoon into a warmed serving dish, sprinkle with the parsley, and serve immediately.

Ingredients SERVES 4

2 tbsp. butter
2 tbsp. olive oil
2 large onions, peeled and
finely sliced
1 tsp. brown sugar
2 garlic cloves, peeled and crushed
8 oz. chorizo, sliced
1 chile, deseeded and finely sliced
14oz. canned chopped tomatoes
1 tbsp. sun-dried tomato paste
$^2/_3$ cup red wine
salt and freshly ground black pepper
4 cups rigatoni
freshly chopped parsley, to garnish

Helpful hint

Although there are many different types of chile, they all have a hot, spicy flavor. Take care when preparing chiles, as the volatile oils in the seeds and the membrane can cause irritation—wash your hands thoroughly afterward.

Chicken Marengo

1 Season the flour with salt and pepper and toss the chicken in the flour to coat. Heat 2 tablespoons of the olive oil in a large skillet and cook the chicken for 7 minutes or until browned, turning occasionally. Remove from the skillet using a slotted spoon and keep warm.

2 Add the remaining oil to the skillet, then add the onion and cook, stirring occasionally, for 5 minutes or until softened and starting to brown. Add the garlic, tomatoes, tomato paste, basil, and thyme. Pour in the wine or chicken stock and season well. Bring to a boil. Stir in the chicken pieces, and simmer for 15 minutes or until the chicken is tender and the sauce has thickened.

3 Meanwhile, bring a large pan of lightly salted water to a boil. Add the rigatoni and cook according to the package directions until tender but still firm to the bite.

4 Drain the rigatoni thoroughly, then return to the pan and stir in the chopped parsley. Tip the pasta into a large, warmed serving dish or spoon onto individual plates. Spoon the chicken sauce over the pasta and serve immediately.

Ingredients   SERVES 4

2 tbsp. all-purpose flour

salt and freshly ground black pepper

4 boneless, skinless chicken breasts, cut into bite-size pieces

4 tbsp. olive oil

1 Spanish onion, peeled and chopped

1 garlic clove, peeled and chopped

14oz. canned chopped tomatoes

2 tbsp. sun-dried tomato paste

3 tbsp. freshly chopped basil

3 tbsp. freshly chopped thyme

$1/_2$ cup dry white wine or chicken stock

3 cups rigatoni

3 tbsp. freshly chopped Italian flat-leaf parsley

Helpful hint

Spanish onions have a milder flavor and tend to be larger than others. Cook the onion over a fairly low heat until really soft, stirring frequently toward the end to keep it from sticking. Let it caramelize and brown very slightly, as this adds a richer flavor and golden color to the final dish.

Creamed Lamb & Wild Mushroom Pasta

1. Place the porcini in a small bowl and cover with almost-boiling water. Let soak for 30 minutes. Drain the porcini, saving the soaking liquid. Chop the porcini finely.

2. Bring a large pan of lightly salted water to a rolling boil. Add the pasta and cook according to the package directions until tender but still firm to the bite.

3. Meanwhile, melt the butter with the olive oil in a large skillet and fry the lamb to seal. Add the garlic, mushrooms, and prepared porcini, and cook for 5 minutes or until just soft.

4. Add the wine and the porcini soaking liquid, then simmer for 2 minutes. Stir in the cream with the seasoning and simmer for 1–2 minutes until just thickened.

5. Drain the pasta thoroughly, setting aside about 4 tablespoons of the cooking water. Return the pasta to the pan. Pour over the mushroom sauce and toss lightly together, adding the pasta water if the sauce is too thick. Spoon into a warmed serving dish or onto individual plates. Garnish with the chopped parsley and serve immediately with grated Parmesan cheese.

Ingredients

SERVES 4

$2/_3$ cup dried porcini
4 cups pasta shapes
2 tbsp. butter
1 tbsp. olive oil
12 oz. lamb neck fillet, thinly sliced
1 garlic clove, peeled and crushed
$2^1/_2$ cups wiped and sliced cremini or
   wild mushrooms
4 tbsp. white wine
$1/_2$ cup heavy cream
salt and freshly ground black pepper
1 tbsp. freshly chopped parsley,
   to garnish
freshly grated Parmesan cheese,
   to serve

Helpful hint

Dried porcini mushrooms have a rich, intense flavor. After soaking, they should be briefly rinsed to remove any grit or dirt. Strain the soaking liquid through a fine strainer. If you do not have this, leave it to settle for about 10 minutes; grit will sink to the bottom and the liquid can be poured off, leaving any sediment behind.

Spicy Chili Beef

1 Heat the olive oil in a large heavy pan. Add the onion and red bell pepper, and cook for 5 minutes or until beginning to soften. Add the ground beef and cook over a high heat for 5–8 minutes until the meat is browned. Stir with a wooden spoon during cooking to break up any lumps in the meat. Add the garlic and chiles, fry for 1 minute, then season to taste.

2 Add the chopped tomatoes, tomato paste, and the kidney beans to the pan. Bring to a boil, lower the heat, and simmer, covered, for at least 40 minutes, stirring occasionally. Stir in the grated chocolate and cook for 3 minutes or until melted.

3 Meanwhile, bring a large pan of lightly salted water to a rolling boil. Add the fusilli and cook according to the package directions until tender but still firm to the bite.

4 Drain the pasta, return to the pan, and toss with the butter and parsley. Spoon into a warmed serving dish or spoon onto individual plates. Spoon the sauce over the pasta. Sprinkle with paprika and serve immediately with spoonfuls of sour cream.

Ingredients SERVES 4

2 tbsp. olive oil
1 onion, peeled and finely chopped
1 red bell pepper, deseeded and sliced
5 cups ground beef
2 garlic cloves, peeled and crushed
2 red chiles, deseeded and finely sliced
salt and freshly ground black pepper
14oz. canned chopped tomatoes
2 tbsp. tomato paste
14oz. canned red kidney beans, drained
2 squares good-quality dark
　chocolate, grated
3 cups dried fusilli
1 tsp. butter
2 tbsp. freshly chopped Italian
　flat-leaf parsley
paprika, to garnish
sour cream, to serve

Food fact

The chocolate in this traditional spicy Mexican dish adds rich, warm undertones, color, and a slight sweetness, but no-one will realize it is there unless you tell them.

Fish & Seafood

Fish is fantastic! Being naturally low in fat and quick to cook makes it a perfect option for a speedy, healthy, and delicious meal. Eat it broiled, stir-fried, baked, or roasted—anything goes. Ratatouille Mackerel is a cheap and tasty option, while Broiled Snapper with Roasted Pepper gives maximum flavor with minimum input. For a bit of a bite, why not try Chili Monkfish Stir-Fry or Coconut Fish Curry?

Sardines with Red Currants

1 Preheat the broiler and line the broiler rack with foil 2–3 minutes before cooking.

2 Warm the red currant jelly in a bowl standing over a pan of gently simmering water and stir until smooth. Add the lime rind and sherry to the bowl, and stir until blended.

3 Lightly rinse the sardines and pat dry with absorbent paper towels. Place on a chopping board and with a sharp knife, make several diagonal cuts across the flesh of each fish. Season the sardines inside the cavities with salt and pepper.

4 Gently brush the warm marinade over the skin and inside the cavities of the sardines.

5 Place on the broiler rack and cook under the preheated broiler for 8–10 minutes until the fish are cooked.

6 Carefully turn the sardines over at least once during broiling. Baste occasionally with the remaining red currant and lime marinade. Garnish with the red currants. Serve immediately with the salad and lime wedges.

Ingredients SERVES 4

2 tbsp. red currant jelly
2 tsp. finely grated lime rind
2 tbsp. medium-dry sherry
1 lb. fresh sardines, cleaned and
    heads removed
sea salt and freshly ground
    black pepper
fresh red currants, to garnish (buy
    frozen if you can't find fresh)

To serve:
fresh green salad
lime wedges

Helpful hint
Most fish are sold cleaned, but it is easy to do yourself. Using the back of a knife, scrape off the scales from the tail toward the head. Using a sharp knife, make a small slit along the belly. Carefully scrape out the entrails and rinse the fish thoroughly under cold running water. Pat dry with absorbent paper towels.

2

3

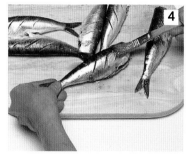
4

Ratatouille Mackerel

1 Preheat the oven to 375°F. Cut the top off the red bell pepper, remove the seeds and membrane, then cut into chunks. Cut the red onion into thick wedges.

2 Heat the oil in a large saucepan, and cook the onion and garlic for 5 minutes or until beginning to soften.

3 Add the bell pepper chunks and zucchini slices, and cook for an additional 5 minutes.

4 Pour in the chopped tomatoes with their juice, and cook for an additional 5 minutes. Season to taste with salt and pepper, and pour into an ovenproof dish.

5 Season the fish with salt and pepper and arrange on top of the vegetables. Spray with a little olive oil and lemon juice. Cover and cook in the preheated oven for 20 minutes.

6 Remove the cover, add the basil leaves, and return to the oven for an additional 5 minutes. Serve immediately with couscous or rice mixed with parsley.

Ingredients   SERVES 4

1 red bell pepper
1 red onion, peeled
1 tbsp. olive oil
1 garlic clove, peeled and thinly sliced
2 zucchini, trimmed and sliced
14oz. canned chopped tomatoes
sea salt and freshly ground
　　black pepper
4 10-oz. small mackerel, cleaned and
　　heads removed
spray olive oil
lemon juice, for drizzling
12 fresh basil leaves
couscous or rice mixed with chopped
　　parsley, to serve

Food fact

Ratatouille is a traditional French dish made with onions, tomatoes, zucchini, and often eggplant. It is a very versatile dish to which many other vegetables can be added. For that extra kick, why not add a little chopped chile?

Teriyaki Salmon

1 Using a sharp knife, cut the salmon into thick slices and place in a shallow dish. Mix together the teriyaki sauce, rice wine vinegar, tomato paste, hot chili sauce, lemon zest, and seasoning. Spoon the marinade over the salmon, then cover loosely and allow to marinate in the refrigerator for 30 minutes, turning the salmon or spooning the marinade over the salmon occasionally.

2 Heat a large wok, then add 2 tablespoons of the oil until almost smoking. Stir-fry the carrot for 2 minutes, then add the snow peas and stir-fry for an additional 2 minutes. Add the mushrooms and stir-fry for 4 minutes until softened. Using a slotted spoon, transfer the vegetables to four warmed serving plates and keep warm.

3 Remove the salmon from the marinade, setting aside both the salmon and marinade. Add the remaining oil to the wok, heat until almost smoking, then cook the salmon for 4–5 minutes, turning once during cooking, until the fish is just flaking. Add the marinade and heat through for 1 minute. Serve immediately with the salmon arranged on top of the vegetables, and the marinade drizzled on top.

Ingredients SERVES 4

1-lb. salmon fillet, skinned
6 tbsp. Japanese teriyaki sauce
1 tbsp. rice wine vinegar
1 tbsp. tomato paste
dash hot chili sauce
2 tsp. grated lemon zest
salt and freshly ground black pepper
$1/4$ cup peanut oil
1 carrot, peeled and cut
    into matchsticks
1 cup snow peas
$1^{1}/_{4}$ cups wiped oyster or
    exotic mushrooms

Tasty tip

Teriyaki sauce is available at stores, but to make your own, mix together 2 tablespoons sake, 2 tablespoons mirin, 2 tablespoons Japanese soy sauce, and 2 tablespoons sugar. Beat together until the sugar has dissolved, and use as above.

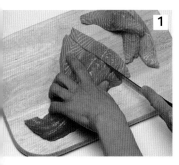

Fresh Tuna Salad

1 Wash the greens and place in a large salad bowl with the cherry tomatoes and arugula, and set aside.

2 Heat the wok, then add the oil and heat until almost smoking. Add the tuna, skin-side down, and cook for 4–6 minutes, turning once during cooking, until cooked and the flesh flakes easily. Remove from the heat and let stand in the juices for 2 minutes before removing.

3 Meanwhile, make the dressing. Place the olive oil, lemon zest, lemon juice, and mustard in a small bowl or screw-topped jar, and beat or shake well until well blended. Season to taste with salt and pepper.

4 Transfer the tuna to a clean chopping board and flake, then add it to the salad and toss lightly.

5 Using a swivel-blade vegetable peeler, peel the piece of Parmesan cheese into shavings. Divide the salad among four large serving plates, drizzle the dressing over the salad, then sprinkle with the Parmesan shavings.

Ingredients   SERVES 4

5 cups mixed greens
2 cups halved lengthwise baby
   cherry tomatoes
$2^{1}/_{2}$ cups washed arugula
2 tbsp. peanut oil
$1^{1}/_{4}$ lbs. boned tuna steaks, each cut
   into 4 small pieces
small piece fresh Parmesan cheese

For the dressing:

$^{1}/_{2}$ cup olive oil
1 tbsp. grated lemon zest
2 tbsp. lemon juice
1 tbsp. mustard
salt and freshly ground black pepper

Helpful hint

Bags of mixed greens are available from all major supermarkets. Although they seem expensive, there is very little waste and they save time. Rinse the leaves before using.

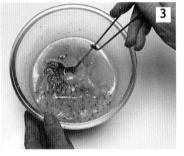

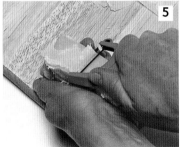

Tuna Fish Burgers

1 Place the potatoes in a large saucepan, cover with boiling water, and simmer until soft. Drain, then mash with 3 tablespoons of the butter and the milk. Turn into a large bowl. Drain the tuna, discarding the oil, and flake into the bowl of potatoes. Stir well to mix.

2 Add the scallion and parsley, and season to taste with salt and pepper. Add 1 tablespoon of the beaten egg to bind the mixture together. Chill in the refrigerator for at least 1 hour.

3 Shape the chilled mixture with your hands into four large patties. First, coat the patties with seasoned flour, then brush them with the remaining beaten egg, allowing any excess to drip back into the bowl. Finally, coat them evenly in the bread crumbs, pressing the crumbs on with your hands, if necessary.

4 Heat a little of the oil in a skillet, and fry the patties for 2–3 minutes on each side, until golden, adding more oil if necessary. Drain on paper towels and serve hot on buns with french fries, mixed salad, and chutney.

Ingredients   MAKES 8

$2^2/_3$ cups peeled and coarsely
   diced potatoes
4 tbsp butter
2 tbsp. milk
14-oz. can tuna in oil
1 scallion, trimmed and
   finely chopped
1 tbsp. freshly chopped parsley
salt and freshly ground black pepper
2 large eggs, beaten
2 tbsp. seasoned all-purpose flour
2 cups fresh white bread crumbs
4 tbsp. vegetable oil
4 hamburger buns

To serve:
french fries
mixed salad
tomato chutney

Helpful hint
Drain the potatoes thoroughly and dry them over a very low heat before mashing to ensure the mixture is not too soft to shape.

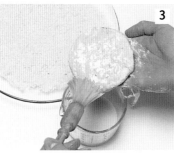

Chili Monkfish Stir-Fry

1   Bring a large saucepan of lightly salted water to a boil and add the pasta. Stir, bring back to a boil, and cook at a rolling boil for 8 minutes or until tender but still firm to the bite. Drain thoroughly and set aside.

2   For the marinade, mix together the sliced garlic, dark soy sauce, lime zest, lime juice, sweet chili sauce, and olive oil in a shallow dish, then add the monkfish chunks. Stir until all the monkfish is lightly coated in the marinade, then cover and leave in the refrigerator for at least 30 minutes, spooning the marinade over the fish occasionally.

3   Heat a wok, then add the oil and heat until almost smoking. Remove the monkfish from the marinade, scraping off as much marinade as possible, add to the wok, and stir-fry for 3 minutes. Add the green chile and sesame seeds, and stir-fry for an additional minute.

4   Stir in the pasta and marinade, and stir-fry for 1–2 minutes until piping hot. Sprinkle with cayenne pepper and garnish with sliced green chiles. Serve immediately.

Ingredients   SERVES 4

$4^1/_2$ cups pasta twists
$1^1/_4$ lbs. monkfish, trimmed and cut
   into chunks
2 tbsp. peanut oil
1 green chile, seeded and cut
   into matchsticks
2 tbsp. sesame seeds
pinch cayenne pepper
sliced green chiles, to garnish

For the marinade:

1 garlic clove, peeled and chopped
2 tbsp. dark soy sauce
2 tsp. grated lime zest
1 tbsp. lime juice
1 tbsp. sweet chili sauce
$^1/_4$ cup olive oil

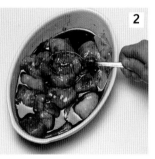

Broiled Goatfish with Orange & Anchovy Sauce

1 Preheat the broiler and line the broiler rack with foil just before cooking. Peel the oranges with a sharp knife over a bowl in order to catch the juice. Cut into thin slices and set aside. If necessary, make up the juice to $^2/_3$ cup with extra orange juice.

2 Place the fish on a chopping board and make two diagonal slashes across the thickest part of both sides of the fish. Season well, both inside and out, with salt and pepper. Tuck a rosemary sprig and a few lemon slices inside the cavity of each fish. Brush the fish with a little of the olive oil and then cook under the preheated broiler for 4–5 minutes on each side. The flesh should just fall away from the bone.

3 Heat the remaining oil in a saucepan, and gently cook the garlic and anchovies for 3–4 minutes. Do not allow to brown. Add the chopped rosemary and plenty of black pepper. The anchovies will be salty enough, so do not add any salt. Stir in the orange slices with their juice and the lemon juice. Simmer gently until heated through. Spoon the sauce over the fish and serve immediately.

Ingredients   SERVES 4

2 oranges
4 goatfish or red snapper, cleaned
  and scaled
salt and freshly ground black pepper
4 fresh rosemary sprigs
1 lemon, sliced
2 tbsp. olive oil
2 garlic cloves, peeled and crushed
6 anchovy fillets in oil, drained and
  coarsely chopped
2 tsp. freshly chopped rosemary
1 tsp. lemon juice

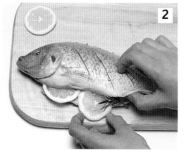

Broiled Snapper with Roasted Pepper

1 Preheat the broiler to a high heat and line the broiler rack with foil. Cut the tops off the bell peppers and divide into quarters. Remove the seeds and the membrane, then place on the foil-lined broiler rack and cook for 8–10 minutes, turning frequently until the skins have become charred and blackened. Remove from the broiler rack, place in a plastic container, and allow to cool. When the bell peppers are cool, strip off the skin, slice thinly, and set aside.

2 Cover the broiler rack with another piece of foil, then place the snapper fillets skin-side up on the broiler rack. Season to taste with salt and pepper and brush with a little of the olive oil. Cook for 10-12 minutes, turning over once and brushing again with a little olive oil.

3 Pour the cream and wine into a small saucepan, bring to a boil, then simmer for about 5 minutes until the sauce has thickened slightly. Add the dill, season to taste, and stir in the sliced bell peppers. Arrange the cooked snapper fillets on warm serving plates, and pour over the cream and pepper sauce. Garnish with sprigs of dill and serve immediately with freshly cooked tagliatelle.

Ingredients SERVES 4

1 medium red bell pepper
1 medium green bell pepper
4–8 snapper fillets, depending on
    size, about 1 lb. total
sea salt and freshly ground
    black pepper
1 tbsp. olive oil
$^1/_3$ cup heavy cream
$^1/_2$ cup white wine
1 tbsp. freshly chopped dill
fresh dill sprigs, to garnish
freshly cooked tagliatelle, to serve

Tasty tip

This dish would be just as tasty with a variety of broiled vegetables—try different-colored bell peppers, red onions, zucchini, and eggplants. Cut into slices or wedges and broil as above. Chop or slice when cool enough to handle.

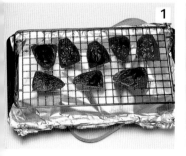

Barbecued Fish Kebabs

1 Line a broiler rack with a single layer of foil, and preheat the broiler. If using wooden skewers, soak in cold water for 30 minutes to keep them from burning during cooking.

2 Meanwhile, prepare the sauce. Add the fish stock, ketchup, Worcestershire sauce, vinegar, sugar, hot chili sauce, and tomato paste to a small saucepan. Stir well and leave to simmer for 5 minutes.

3 When ready to cook, drain the skewers, if necessary, then thread the fish chunks, the quartered red onions, and the cherry tomatoes alternately onto the skewers.

4 Season the kebabs to taste with salt and pepper, and brush with the sauce. Broil under the preheated broiler for 8–10 minutes, basting with the sauce occasionally during cooking. Turn the kebabs often to ensure that they are cooked thoroughly and evenly on all sides. Serve immediately with couscous.

Ingredients SERVES 4

1 lb. herring or mackerel fillets, cut
    into chunks
2 small red onions, peeled
    and quartered
16 cherry tomatoes
salt and freshly ground
    black pepper
couscous, to serve

For the sauce:

$^2/_3$ cup fish stock
5 tbsp. ketchup
2 tbsp. Worcestershire sauce
2 tbsp. wine vinegar
2 tbsp. brown sugar
2 drops hot chili sauce
2 tbsp. tomato paste

Tasty tip

This dish would be ideal for a light summertime evening meal. Instead of cooking indoors, cook these kebabs on the barbecue for a delicious charcoaled flavor.

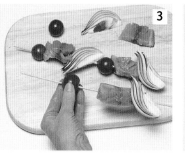

Coconut Fish Curry

1 Put 1 tablespoon of the oil into a large skillet and cook the onion, pepper, and garlic for 5 minutes or until soft. Add the remaining oil, curry paste, ginger, and chile, and cook for an additional minute.

2 Pour in the coconut milk and bring to a boil. Reduce the heat and simmer gently for 5 minutes, stirring occasionally. Add the fish to the pan and continue to simmer gently for 5–10 minutes until the fish is tender, but not overcooked.

3 Meanwhile, cook the rice in a saucepan of salted boiling water for 15 minutes or until tender. Drain the rice thoroughly and turn out into a serving dish.

4 Stir the chopped cilantro and chutney gently into the fish curry, and season to taste with salt and pepper. Spoon the fish curry over the cooked rice, garnish with lime wedges and cilantro sprigs, and serve immediately with spoonfuls of plain yogurt and warm naan bread.

Ingredients   SERVES 4

2 tbsp. sunflower oil

1 medium onion, peeled and very finely chopped

1 yellow bell pepper, deseeded and finely chopped

1 garlic clove, peeled and crushed

1 tbsp. mild curry paste

1-in. piece ginger, peeled and grated

1 red chile, deseeded and finely chopped

14oz. canned coconut milk

$1\frac{1}{2}$ lb. firm white fish, skinned and cut into chunks

$1\frac{1}{3}$ cups basmati rice

1 tbsp. freshly chopped cilantro

1 tbsp. mango chutney

salt and freshly ground black pepper

To garnish:
lime wedges
fresh cilantro sprigs

To serve:
plain yogurt
warm naan bread

Haddock with an Olive Crust

1 Preheat the oven to 375°F. Place the olives in a small bowl with the bread crumbs, and add the chopped tarragon.

2 Add the crushed garlic to the olives with the chopped scallions and the olive oil. Mix together lightly.

3 Wipe the fillets with either a clean, damp cloth or damp paper towels, then place on a lightly greased baking sheet.

4 Place spoonfuls of the olive and bread crumb mixture on top of each fillet, and press the mixture down lightly and evenly over the top of the fish

5 Bake the fish in the preheated oven for 20–25 minutes until the fish is cooked thoroughly, and the topping is golden brown. Serve immediately with the freshly cooked carrots and beans.

Ingredients SERVES 4

12 pitted ripe olives, finely chopped
$^3/_4$ cup fresh white bread crumbs
1 tbsp. freshly chopped tarragon
1 garlic clove, peeled and crushed
3 scallions, trimmed and
   finely chopped
1 tbsp. olive oil
4 thick, skinless haddock fillets,
   6 oz. each

To serve:
freshly cooked carrots
freshly cooked beans

Tasty tip
Why not try experimenting by adding other ingredients to the crust? Adding 2 cloves of roasted garlic gives the crust a delicious flavor. Simply mash the garlic and add to the crumbs. Also, a combination of white and whole-wheat bread crumbs can be used for a nuttier, malty taste.

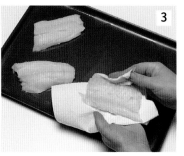

Gingered Cod Steaks

1 Preheat the broiler and line the broiler rack with a layer of foil. Coarsely grate the piece of fresh ginger. Trim the scallions and cut into thin strips.

2 Mix the scallions, ginger, chopped parsley, and sugar together. Add 1 tablespoon of water.

3 Wipe the fish steaks. Season to taste with salt and pepper. Place onto four separate 8 x 8 inch foil squares.

4 Carefully spoon the scallions and ginger mixture evenly over the fish.

5 Cut the butter into small cubes and place over the fish.

6 Loosely fold the foil over the steaks to enclose the fish and to make a pocket.

7 Place under the preheated broiler and cook for 10–12 minutes until cooked and the flesh has turned opaque.

8 Place the fish pockets on individual serving plates. Serve immediately with the freshly cooked vegetables.

Ingredients   SERVES 4

1-in. piece fresh ginger, peeled
4 scallions
2 tsp. freshly chopped parsley
1 tbsp. brown sugar
4 6-oz. cod steaks
salt and freshly ground
    black pepper
2 tbsp. reduced-fat butter
freshly cooked vegetables,
    to serve

Tasty tip

Why not serve this dish with roasted new potatoes en papillote? Place the new potatoes into double-thickness paper with a few cloves of peeled garlic. Drizzle with a little olive oil and season well with salt and black pepper. Fold all the edges of the waxed paper together, and roast in the preheated oven at 350°F for 40–50 minutes before serving in the paper casing.

Seared Pancetta-Wrapped Cod

1 Wipe the cod fillets and wrap each one with the pancetta. Secure each fillet with a toothpick and set aside.

2 Drain the capers and soak in cold water for 10 minutes to remove any excess salt, then drain and set aside.

3 Heat the oil in a large skillet and sear the wrapped pieces of cod fillet for about 3 minutes on each side, turning carefully with a spatula so as not to break up the fish.

4 Lower the heat, then continue to cook for 2–3 minutes until the fish is cooked thoroughly.

5 Meanwhile, place the remaining capers, lemon juice, and olive oil in a small saucepan. Add the black pepper.

6 Place the saucepan over a low heat and bring to a gentle simmer, stirring continuously for 2–3 minutes.

7 Once the fish is cooked, garnish with the parsley and serve with the warm caper dressing, freshly cooked vegetables, and new potatoes.

Ingredients   SERVES 4

4 6-oz. cod fillets
4 very thin slices pancetta
3 tbsp. capers, in vinegar
1 tbsp. vegetable or corn oil
2 tbsp. lemon juice
1 tbsp. olive oil
freshly ground black pepper
1 tbsp. freshly chopped parsley,
    to garnish

To serve:

freshly cooked vegetables
new potatoes

Food fact

Pancetta is Italian-cured belly pork, which is often delicately smoked and sold either finely sliced or chopped coarsely into small cubes. The slices of pancetta can be used to encase poultry and fish, whereas chopped pancetta is often used in sauces. To cook chopped pancetta, fry for 2–3 minutes and set aside. Use the oil to seal meat or fry onions, then return pancetta to the pan.

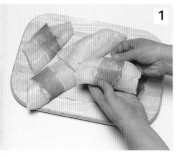

1

3

6

Citrus-Broiled Flounder

1 Heat the oil in a large skillet, then cook the onion, bell pepper, and rice for 2 minutes.

2 Add the orange and lemon juice, and bring to a boil. Reduce the heat, add half the stock, and simmer for 15–20 minutes until the rice is tender, adding the remaining stock as necessary.

3 Preheat the broiler. Finely spray the base of the broiler pan with oil. Place the flounder fillets in the base and set aside.

4 Finely grate the orange and lemon zest. Squeeze the juice from half of each fruit.

5 Melt the butter or low-fat spread in a small saucepan. Add the grated zest, juice, and half of the tarragon, and use to baste the flounder fillets.

6 Cook one side only of the fish under the preheated broiler at a medium heat for 4–6 minutes, basting continuously.

7 Once the rice is cooked, stir in the remaining tarragon, and season to taste with salt and pepper. Garnish the fish with the lemon wedges, and serve immediately with the rice.

Ingredients   SERVES 4

1 tsp. corn oil
1 onion, peeled and chopped
1 orange bell pepper, seeded
    and chopped
$^3/_4$ cup long-grain rice
$^2/_3$ cup orange juice
2 tbsp. lemon juice
1 cup vegetable stock
spray oil
4 6-oz. flounder fillets, skinned
1 orange
1 lemon
2 tbsp. reduced-fat butter
    or low-fat spread
2 tbsp. freshly chopped tarragon
salt and freshly ground black pepper
lemon wedges, to garnish

Tasty tip

Flounder is caught mainly in cold Atlantic waters. It can be bought fresh or frozen, whole or in fillets, and can be fried, poached, or broiled. Sole or halibut can be used in place of flounder, but they are more expensive.

Chunky Fish Casserole

1 Melt the butter or margarine in a large saucepan, add the onions and pepper, and cook for 5 minutes or until softened.

2 Cut the peeled potatoes into 1-in. cubes, rinse lightly, and shake dry, then add them to the onions and pepper in the saucepan. Add the zucchini and cook, stirring frequently, for an additional 2–3 minutes.

3 Sprinkle the flour, paprika, and vegetable oil into the saucepan and cook, stirring continuously, for 1 minute. Pour in $^2/_3$ cup of the wine, with all the stock, and the chopped tomatoes, and bring to a boil.

4 Add the basil to the casserole, season to taste with salt and pepper, and cover. Simmer for 15 minutes, then add the fish and the remaining wine, and simmer very gently for an additional 5–7 minutes, until the fish and vegetables are just tender. Garnish with basil sprigs and serve immediately with freshly cooked rice.

Ingredients   SERVES 6

4 tbsp. butter or margarine
2 large onions, peeled and sliced
    into rings
1 red bell pepper, deseeded and
    roughly chopped
1 lb. potatoes, peeled
1 lb. zucchini, trimmed and
    thickly sliced
2 tbsp. all-purpose flour
1 tbsp. paprika
2 tsp. vegetable oil
$1^1/_4$ cups white wine
$^2/_3$ cup fish stock
14oz. canned chopped tomatoes
2 tbsp. freshly chopped basil
salt and freshly ground black pepper
1 lb. firm white fish fillet, skinned and
    cut into 1-in. cubes
fresh basil sprigs, to garnish
freshly cooked rice, to serve

Food fact

Halibut is a flatfish with firm, milky white flesh that has an almost meaty texture, making it ideal for this casserole.

Crispy Shrimp Stir-Fry

1 Mix together the soy sauce, cornstarch, and sugar in a small bowl, and set aside.

2 Heat a large wok, then add 3 tablespoons of the oil, and heat until almost smoking. Add the shrimp and stir-fry for 4 minutes or until pink all over. Using a slotted spoon, transfer the shrimp to a plate and set aside in a warm oven.

3 Add the remaining oil to the wok, and when just smoking, add the carrots and ginger, and stir-fry for 1 minute or until slightly softened, then add the snow peas and stir-fry for an additional minute. Add the asparagus and stir-fry for 4 minutes or until softened.

4 Add the bean sprouts and Chinese cabbage, and stir-fry for 2 minutes or until the cabbage is slightly wilted. Pour in the soy sauce mixture and return the shrimp to the wok. Stir-fry over a medium heat until piping hot, then add the sesame oil, give a final stir, and serve immediately.

Ingredients　　SERVES 4

3 tbsp. soy sauce

1 tsp. cornstarch

pinch sugar

6 tbsp. peanut oil

1 lb. raw shelled jumbo shrimp, halved lengthwise

$^{3}/_{4}$ cup peeled and cut carrots

1-in. piece fresh ginger, peeled and cut into matchsticks

1 cup trimmed and shredded snow peas

$^{1}/_{4}$ cup halved asparagus spears

$^{3}/_{4}$ cup bean sprouts

$^{1}/_{4}$ head Chinese cabbage or bok choy, shredded

2 tsp. sesame oil

Helpful hint

As always with wok cooking, good preparation saves a lot of time. It is essential to cut everything into small, uniform pieces and have everything ready before starting to cook.

Coconut Seafood

1 Heat a large wok, add the oil, and heat until it is almost smoking, swirling the oil around the wok to coat the sides. Add the shrimp and stir-fry over a high heat for 4–5 minutes until browned on all sides. Using a slotted spoon, transfer the shrimp to a plate and set aside in a warm oven.

2 Add the scallions, garlic, and ginger to the wok, and stir-fry for 1 minute. Add the mushrooms and stir-fry for an additional 3 minutes. Using a slotted spoon, transfer the mushroom mixture to a plate and set aside in the warm oven.

3 Add the wine and coconut milk to the wok, bring to a boil, and boil rapidly for 4 minutes until reduced slightly.

4 Return the mushroom mixture and shrimp to the wok, bring back to a boil, then simmer for 1 minute, stirring occasionally, until piping hot. Stir in the freshly chopped cilantro and season to taste with salt and pepper. Serve immediately with the freshly cooked Thai fragrant rice.

Ingredients SERVES 4

2 tbsp. peanut oil
1 lb. raw jumbo shrimp, shelled
2 bunches scallions, trimmed and
   thickly sliced
1 garlic clove, peeled and chopped
1-in. piece fresh ginger, peeled and
   cut into matchsticks
1 cup rinsed and halved fresh
   shiitake mushrooms
$^2/_3$ cup dry white wine
1 cup coconut milk
4 tbsp. freshly chopped cilantro
salt and freshly ground black pepper
freshly cooked Thai fragrant rice

Helpful hint

If coconut milk is not available, shred $^1/_2$ cup creamed coconut into $^1/_4$ cup of hot water. Beat until completely dissolved, and use as above.

Mussels with Creamy Garlic & Saffron Sauce

1 Clean the mussels thoroughly in plenty of cold water and remove any beards and barnacles from the shells. Discard any mussels that are open or damaged. Place in a large bowl, cover with cold water, and leave in the refrigerator until needed.

2 Pour the wine into a large saucepan and bring to a boil. Tip the mussels into the saucepan, cover, and cook, shaking the pan periodically, for 6–8 minutes until the mussels have opened completely.

3 Discard any mussels with closed shells, then using a slotted spoon, carefully remove the remaining open mussels from the saucepan and keep them warm. Set the cooking liquid aside.

4 Heat the olive oil in a small skillet, and cook the shallot and garlic gently for 2–3 minutes until softened. Add the cooking liquid and chopped oregano, and cook for an additional 3–4 minutes. Stir in the saffron and the cream, and heat through gently. Season to taste with salt and pepper. Place a few mussels in individual serving bowls and spoon over the saffron sauce. Serve immediately with plenty of crusty bread.

Ingredients SERVES 4

$1^1/_2$ lbs. fresh live mussels
$1^1/_4$ cups good-quality dry white wine
1 tbsp. olive oil
1 shallot, peeled and finely chopped
2 garlic cloves, peeled and crushed
1 tbsp. freshly chopped oregano
2 saffron strands
$^2/_3$ cup light cream
salt and freshly ground black pepper
crusty bread, to serve

Helpful hint

Mussels are now farmed and are available most of the year. However, always try to buy mussels the day you intend to eat them. Place them in a bowl of cold water in the refrigerator as soon as possible, changing the water at least every 2 hours. If live mussels are unavailable, use prepacked, cooked mussels.

Thai Crab Cakes

1 Place the crabmeat in a bowl with the ground coriander, chili powder, turmeric, lime juice, sugar, ginger, chopped cilantro, lemongrass, flour, and egg yolks. Mix together well.

2 Divide the mixture into 12 equal portions and form each into a small patty about 2 in. across. Lightly whisk the egg whites and put into a dish. Place the bread crumbs on a separate plate.

3 Dip each crab cake in the egg whites, then in the bread crumbs, turning to coat both sides. Place on a plate, cover, and chill in the refrigerator until ready to cook.

4 Heat the oil in a large skillet. Add six crab cakes and cook for 3 minutes on each side or until crisp, golden brown on the outside, and cooked through. Remove, drain on paper towels, and keep warm while cooking the remaining cakes. Arrange on plates, garnish with lime wedges, and serve immediately with lettuce leaves.

Ingredients SERVES 4

1 cup white and brown crabmeat
1 tsp. ground coriander
$\frac{1}{4}$ tsp. chili powder
$\frac{1}{4}$ tsp. ground turmeric
2 tsp. lime juice
1 tsp. light brown sugar
1-in. piece ginger, peeled and grated
3 tbsp. freshly chopped cilantro
2 tsp. finely chopped lemongrass
2 tbsp all-purpose flour
2 large eggs, separated
1 cup fresh white bread crumbs
3 tbsp. peanut oil
lime wedges, to garnish
mixed lettuce leaves, to serve

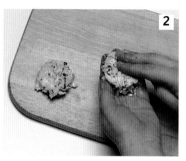

Poultry & Meat

Speedy stir-fries, mouthwatering casseroles, warming bakes: any of this selection of dishes is perfect for a simple, appetizing supper. Stir-Fried Lemon Chicken will fill your kitchen with a divine citrus tang and Beef with Paprika is a sure-fire winner. Family favorites Pork Sausages with Onion Gravy & Best-Ever Mashed Potatoes and Shepherd's Pie will have the kids clamoring for more!

Aromatic Chicken Curry

1 Put the lentils in a sieve and rinse thoroughly under cold running water.

2 Fry the ground coriander and cumin seeds in a large saucepan over a low heat for about 30 seconds. Stir in the curry paste.

3 Add the lentils to the saucepan with the bay leaf and lemon rind, then pour in the stock.

4 Stir, then slowly bring to a boil. Turn down the heat, half-cover the saucepan with a lid, and simmer gently for 5 minutes, stirring occasionally.

5 Secure the chicken thighs with toothpicks to hold their shape. Place in the saucepan and half-cover. Simmer for 15 minutes.

6 Stir in the shredded spinach, and cook for an additional 25 minutes or until the chicken is very tender, and the sauce is thick.

7 Remove the bay leaf and lemon rind. Stir in the cilantro and lemon juice, then season to taste with salt and pepper. Serve immediately with the rice and some plain yogurt.

Ingredients
SERVES 4

$^2/_3$ cup red lentils
2 tsp. ground coriander
$^1/_2$ tsp. cumin seeds
2 tsp. mild curry paste
1 bay leaf
small strip lemon rind
$2^1/_2$ cups chicken or
   vegetable stock
8 chicken thighs, skinned
$^3/_4$ cup rinsed and shredded
   spinach leaves
1 tbsp. freshly chopped cilantro
2 tsp. lemon juice
salt and freshly ground black pepper

To serve:
freshly cooked rice
low-fat plain yogurt

Helpful hint
Frying spices really releases their flavor and is a technique that can be used in many dishes. It is a particularly good way to flavor lean meat or fish.

Stir-Fried Lemon Chicken

1 Using a sharp knife, trim the chicken, discarding any fat, and cut into thin strips, about 2 in. long and $^1/_2$ in. wide. Place in a shallow dish. Lightly whisk the egg white and 1 tablespoon of the cornstarch together until smooth. Pour over the chicken strips and mix well until coated evenly. Leave to marinate in the refrigerator for at least 20 minutes.

2 When ready to cook, drain the chicken and set aside. Heat a wok or large skillet, add the oil, and, when hot, add the chicken and stir-fry for 1–2 minutes until the chicken has turned white. Using a slotted spoon, remove from the wok, and set aside.

3 Wipe the wok clean and return to the heat. Add the chicken stock, lemon juice, soy sauce, Chinese rice wine or sherry, sugar, garlic, and chili flakes, and bring to a boil. Blend the remaining cornstarch with 1 tablespoon of water, and stir into the stock. Simmer for 1 minute.

4 Return the chicken to the wok, and continue simmering for an additional 2–3 minutes until the chicken is tender and the sauce has thickened. Garnish with lemon zest strips and red chile slices. Serve immediately.

Ingredients   SERVES 4

$^3/_4$ lb. boneless, skinless
    chicken breast
1 extra-large egg white
5 tsp. cornstarch
3 tbsp. vegetable or peanut oil
$^2/_3$ cup chicken stock
2 tbsp. fresh lemon juice
2 tbsp. light soy sauce
1 tbsp. Chinese rice wine or
    dry sherry
1 tbsp. sugar
2 garlic cloves, peeled and
    finely chopped
$^1/_4$ tsp. dried chili flakes, or to taste

To garnish:
lemon zest strips
red chile slices

Food fact

Chili flakes are crushed, dried red chiles and are widely used in parts of China, where long strings of red chiles can be seen drying in the sun.

Soy-Glazed Chicken Thighs

1 Heat a large wok and, when hot, add the oil. Stir-fry the chicken thighs for 5 minutes or until golden. Remove and drain on absorbent paper towels. You may need to do this in two or three batches.

2 Pour off the oil and fat and, using absorbent paper towels, carefully wipe out the wok. Add the garlic, along with the ginger, soy sauce, Chinese rice wine or sherry, and honey to the wok and stir well. Sprinkle in the brown sugar with the hot chili sauce to taste, then place over the heat and bring to a boil.

3 Reduce the heat to a gentle simmer, then carefully add the chicken thighs. Cover the wok and simmer gently over a very low heat for 30 minutes or until they are tender and the sauce is reduced and thickened, and glazes the chicken thighs.

4 Stir or spoon the sauce occasionally over the chicken thighs and add a little water if the sauce is starting to become too thick. Arrange in a shallow serving dish, garnish with freshly chopped parsley, and serve immediately.

Ingredients SERVES 6–8

2 tbsp. vegetable oil
2 lbs. chicken thighs
3–4 garlic cloves, peeled and crushed
$1\frac{1}{2}$-in. piece fresh ginger, peeled and finely chopped or grated
$\frac{1}{2}$ cup soy sauce
2–3 tbsp. Chinese rice wine or dry sherry
2 tbsp. honey
1 tbsp. brown sugar
2–3 dashes hot chili sauce, or to taste
freshly chopped parsley, to garnish

Tasty tip

Often overlooked, chicken wings are inexpensive and very flavorful. Served this way, with a sticky coating, they make an ideal snack. Serve with finger bowls.

Chicken with Porcini Mushrooms & Cream

1   Heat the olive oil in a large heavy skillet, then add the chicken breasts, skin-side down, and cook for about 10 minutes until they are well browned. Remove the chicken breasts and set aside. Add the garlic, stir into the juices, and cook for 1 minute.

2   Pour the vermouth or white wine into the skillet, and season to taste with salt and pepper. Return the chicken to the skillet. Bring to a boil, reduce the heat to low, and simmer for about 20 minutes until tender.

3   In another large skillet, heat the butter and add the sliced porcini or wild mushrooms. Stir-fry for about 5 minutes until the mushrooms are golden and tender.

4   Add the porcini or wild mushrooms and any juices to the chicken. Season to taste with salt and pepper, then add the chopped oregano. Stir together gently and cook for 1 minute longer. Transfer to a large serving plate, and garnish with sprigs of fresh basil, if desired. Serve immediately with rice.

Ingredients   SERVES 4

2 tbsp. olive oil
4 boneless chicken breasts
2 garlic cloves, peeled and crushed
$2/3$ cup dry vermouth or dry
   white wine
salt and freshly ground black pepper
2 tbsp. butter
4 cups thickly sliced porcini or
   wild mushrooms,
1 tbsp. freshly chopped oregano
fresh basil sprigs, to garnish
freshly cooked rice, to serve

Helpful hint

If using dried mushrooms, cover with almost-boiling water, leave for 20 minutes, then drain, straining the soaking liquid to use.

Chicken Basquaise

1. Dry the chicken pieces well with paper towels. Put the flour in a plastic bag, season with salt and pepper, and add the chicken pieces. Twist the bag to seal, then shake to coat the chicken pieces thoroughly. Heat 2 tablespoons of the oil in a large heavy saucepan over a medium-high heat. Add the chicken pieces and cook for about 15 minutes, turning on all sides, until well browned. Using a slotted spoon, transfer to a plate.

2. Add the remaining olive oil to the saucepan, then add the onion and bell peppers. Reduce the heat to medium and cook, stirring frequently, until starting to brown and soften. Stir in the garlic and chorizo, and continue cooking for an additional 3 minutes. Add the rice and cook for about 2 minutes, stirring to coat with the oil, until the rice is translucent and golden.

3. Stir in the stock, crushed chiles, thyme, tomato paste, and salt and pepper, and bring to a boil. Return the chicken to the saucepan, pressing it gently into the rice. Cover and cook over a very low heat for about 45 minutes until the chicken and rice are cooked and tender.

4. Gently stir in the ham, ripe olives, and half the parsley. Cover and heat for an additional 5 minutes. Sprinkle with the remaining parsley and serve immediately.

Ingredients   SERVES 4–6

3 lb. chicken, cut into 8 pieces

2 tbsp. all-purpose flour

salt and freshly ground black pepper

3 tbsp. olive oil

1 large onion, peeled and sliced

2 red bell peppers, deseeded and cut into thick strips

2 garlic cloves, peeled and crushed

$1/4$ lb. spicy chorizo sausage, cut into $1/2$-in. pieces

heaping 1 cup long-grain white rice

2 cups chicken stock

1 tsp. crushed dried chiles

$1/2$ tsp. dried thyme

1 tbsp. tomato paste

$1^{1}/_{4}$ cups diced Spanish ham

12 ripe olives

2 tbsp. freshly chopped parsley

Braised Chicken in Beer

1 Preheat the oven to 325°F. Cut each chicken joint in half and put in an ovenproof casserole dish with the prunes and bay leaves.

2 To peel the shallots, put in a small bowl and cover with boiling water. After 2 minutes, drain the shallots and rinse under cold water until cool enough to handle. The skins should then peel away easily from the shallots. Heat the oil in a large nonstick skillet. Add the shallots and cook gently for about 5 minutes until beginning to brown.

3 Add the mushrooms to the skillet and cook for an additional 3–4 minutes until both the mushrooms and onions are softened.

4 Sprinkle the sugar over the shallots and mushrooms, then add the mustard, tomato paste, beer, and chicken stock. Season to taste with salt and pepper, and bring to a boil, stirring to combine. Carefully pour over the chicken. Cover the casserole and cook in the preheated oven for 1 hour. Blend the cornstarch with the lemon juice and 1 tablespoon of cold water, and stir into the chicken casserole. Return to the oven for an additional 10 minutes until the chicken is cooked and the vegetables are tender. Remove the bay leaves and stir in the chopped parsley. Garnish the chicken with the Italian flat-leaf parsley. Serve with the mashed potatoes and green vegetables.

Ingredients SERVES 4

4 chicken joints, skinned
$^2/_3$ cup pitted dried prunes
2 bay leaves
12 shallots
2 tsp. olive oil
$1^3/_4$ cups wiped small button
    mushrooms
1 tsp. dark brown sugar
$^1/_2$ tsp. mustard
2 tsp. tomato paste
$^2/_3$ cup light beer
$^2/_3$ cup chicken stock
salt and freshly ground black pepper
2 tsp. cornstarch
2 tsp. lemon juice
2 tbsp. freshly chopped parsley
Italian flat-leaf parsley, to garnish

To serve:

mashed potatoes
seasonal green vegetables

Turkey & Oven-Roasted Vegetable Salad

1 Preheat the oven to 400°F. Line a large roasting pan with foil, then pour in half the olive oil and place in the oven for 3 minutes or until very hot. Remove from the oven, add the zucchini and bell peppers, and stir until evenly coated. Roast for 30–35 minutes until slightly charred, turning occasionally.

2 Add the pine nuts to the pan. Return to the oven and roast for 10 minutes or until the pine nuts are toasted. Remove from the oven and let the vegetables cool completely.

3 Bring a large pan of lightly salted water to a rolling boil. Add the macaroni and cook according to the package directions until tender but still firm to the bite. Drain and rinse the pasta under cold running water, then drain thoroughly and place in a large salad bowl.

4 Cut the turkey into bite-size pieces and add to the macaroni. Add the artichokes and tomatoes with the cooled vegetables and pan juices to the pan. Blend together the cilantro, garlic, remaining oil, vinegar, and seasoning. Pour over the salad, then toss lightly and serve.

Ingredients   SERVES 4

6 tbsp. olive oil

3 medium zucchini, trimmed and sliced

2 yellow bell peppers, deseeded and sliced

$1/2$ cup pine nuts

$2^1/_2$ cups macaroni

12 oz. cooked turkey

10 oz. canned chargrilled artichokes, drained and sliced

8 oz. baby plum tomatoes, quartered

4 tbsp. freshly chopped cilantro

1 garlic clove, peeled and chopped

3 tbsp. balsamic vinegar

salt and freshly ground black pepper

Helpful hint

Other vegetables would be equally delicious. Try baby eggplants, trimmed and quartered lengthwise. If you cannot find chargrilled artichokes, use ordinary ones: drain and pat dry, then add to 1 tablespoon of hot olive oil in a skillet and cook for 2–3 minutes.

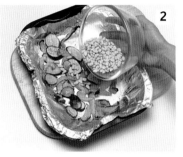
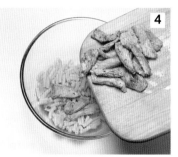

Turkey Tetrazzini

1 Preheat the oven to 350°F. Lightly grease a large ovenproof dish. Bring a large saucepan of lightly salted water to a boil. Add the tagliatelle and cook for 7–9 minutes until tender but still firm to the bite. Drain well and set aside.

2 In a heavy saucepan, heat the butter and add the bacon. Cook for 2–3 minutes until crisp and golden. Add the onion and mushrooms, and cook for 3–4 minutes until the vegetables are tender.

3 Stir in the flour and cook for 2 minutes. Remove from the heat and slowly stir in the stock. Return to the heat and cook, stirring, until a smooth, thick sauce has formed. Add the tagliatelle, then pour in the cream and sherry. Add the turkey and parsley. Season to taste with the nutmeg, salt, and pepper. Toss well to coat.

4 Turn the mixture into the prepared dish, spreading evenly. Sprinkle the top with the Parmesan cheese, and cook in the preheated oven for 30–35 minutes until crisp, golden, and bubbling. Garnish with chopped parsley and Parmesan cheese. Serve straight from the dish.

Ingredients   SERVES 4

3³/₄ cups green and white tagliatelle
4 tbsp. butter
4 slices bacon, diced
1 onion, peeled and finely chopped
1¹/₂ cups thinly sliced mushrooms
¹/₂ cup all-purpose flour
2 cups chicken stock
¹/₂ cup heavy cream
2 tbsp. sherry
5 cups bite-size cooked turkey
    meat pieces,
1 tbsp. freshly chopped parsley
freshly grated nutmeg
salt and freshly ground black pepper
¹/₄ cup grated Parmesan cheese

To garnish:

freshly chopped parsley
Parmesan cheese, grated

Tasty tip

This is a great way to use Thanksgiving leftovers—it's worth putting extra meat in the freezer. Use frozen leftovers within 1 month.

Duck with Berry Sauce

1 Remove the skins from the duck breasts and season with a little salt and pepper. Brush a griddle pan with the oil, then heat on the stove until smoking hot.

2 Place the duck skinned-side down in the pan. Cook over a medium-high heat for 5 minutes or until well browned. Turn the duck and cook for 2 minutes. Lower the heat and cook for an additional 5–8 minutes until cooked, but still slightly pink in the center. Remove from the pan and keep warm.

3 While the duck is cooking, make the sauce. Put the orange juice, bay leaf, red currant jelly, fresh or frozen and dried berries, and sugar in a small griddle pan. Add any juices left in the griddle pan to the small pan. Slowly bring to a boil, lower the heat, and simmer uncovered for 4–5 minutes until the fruit is soft.

4 Remove the bay leaf. Stir in the vinegar and chopped mint, and season to taste with salt and pepper.

5 Slice the duck breasts diagonally, and arrange on serving plates. Spoon the berry sauce on top, and garnish with sprigs of fresh mint. Serve immediately with the potatoes and green beans.

Ingredients   SERVES 4

4 boneless duck breasts, $^1/_2$ lb. each
salt and freshly ground black pepper
1 tsp. corn oil

For the sauce:

$^1/_3$ cup orange juice
1 bay leaf
3 tbsp. red currant jelly
$^3/_4$ cup fresh or frozen
    mixed berries
2 tbsp. dried cranberries or cherries
$^1/_2$ tsp. light brown sugar
1 tbsp. balsamic vinegar
1 tsp. freshly chopped mint
fresh mint sprigs, to garnish

To serve:

freshly cooked potatoes
freshly cooked green beans

Helpful hint

Duck breasts are best served slightly pink in the center. Whole ducks, however, should be thoroughly cooked.

Pork Sausages with Onion Gravy & Best-Ever Mash

1 Melt the butter with the oil and add the onions. Cover and cook gently for about 20 minutes until the onions have collapsed. Add the sugar and stir well. Uncover and continue to cook, stirring often, until the onions are very soft and golden. Add the thyme, stir well, then add the flour while stirring. Gradually add the Madeira and the stock. Bring to a boil and simmer gently for 10 minutes.

2 Meanwhile, put the sausages in a large skillet, and cook over a medium heat for about 15–20 minutes, turning often, until golden brown and slightly sticky all over.

3 For the mashed potatoes, boil the potatoes in plenty of lightly salted water for 15–18 minutes until tender. Drain well and return to the saucepan. Put over a low heat to allow to dry. Remove from the heat and add the butter, crème fraîche or sour cream, and salt and pepper. Mash thoroughly. Serve the mashed potatoes topped with the sausages and onion gravy.

Ingredients SERVES 4

4 tbsp. butter
1 tbsp. olive oil
2 large onions, peeled and thinly sliced
pinch sugar
1 tbsp. freshly chopped thyme
1 tbsp. all-purpose flour
$^1/_2$ cup Madeira
$^3/_4$ cup vegetable stock
8–12 good-quality pork sausages, depending on size

For the mashed potatoes:

2 lbs. floury potatoes, peeled
6 tbsp. butter
4 tbsp. crème fraîche or sour cream
salt and freshly ground black pepper

Helpful hint
Sausages should always be cooked slowly over a gentle heat to ensure that they are cooked through.

Speedy Pork with Yellow Bean Sauce

1 Remove any fat or sinew from the pork fillet, and cut into thin strips. Blend the soy sauce, orange juice, and cornstarch in a bowl and mix thoroughly. Place the meat in a shallow dish, pour over the soy sauce mixture, cover and allow to marinate in the refrigerator for 1 hour. Drain with a slotted spoon, setting the marinade aside.

2 Heat the wok, then add 2 tablespoons of the oil and stir-fry the pork with the garlic for 2 minutes or until the meat is sealed. Remove with a slotted spoon and set aside.

3 Add the remaining oil to the wok and cook the carrots, beans, and scallions for about 3 minutes until tender but still crisp. Return the pork to the wok with the reserved marinade, then pour over the yellow bean sauce. Stir-fry for an additional 1–2 minutes until the pork is tender. Sprinkle with the chopped parsley and serve immediately with freshly cooked egg noodles.

Ingredients SERVES 4

1 lb. pork fillet
2 tbsp. light soy sauce
2 tbsp. orange juice
2 tsp. cornstarch
3 tbsp. peanut oil
2 garlic cloves, peeled and crushed
1 cup peeled and cut carrots
$^3/_4$ cup trimmed and halved fine green beans
2 scallions, trimmed and cut into strips
4 tbsp. yellow bean sauce
1 tbsp. freshly chopped Italian flat-leaf parsley, to garnish
freshly cooked egg noodles, to serve

Food fact

Yellow bean sauce is available from large supermarkets or Asian grocery stores. It is one of many readymade sauces commonly used in Chinese cooking. Black bean sauce may be substituted.

Cashew & Pork Stir-Fry

1 Using a sharp knife, trim the pork, discarding any sinew or fat. Cut into $^3/_4$-in. slices, and place in a shallow dish. Blend the soy sauce and cornstarch together until smooth and free from lumps, then pour over the pork. Stir until coated in the cornstarch mixture, then cover with plastic wrap, and leave to marinate in the refrigerator for at least 30 minutes.

2 Heat a nonstick skillet until hot, add the cashews, and fry for 2–3 minutes until toasted, stirring frequently. Transfer to a plate and set aside.

3 Heat a wok or large skillet, add 2 tablespoons of the oil, and, when hot, add the leeks, ginger, garlic, and bell pepper, and stir-fry for 5 minutes or until softened. Using a slotted spoon, transfer to a plate and keep warm.

4 Drain the pork, setting aside the marinade. Add the remaining oil to the wok and, when hot, add the pork and stir-fry for 5 minutes or until browned. Return the vegetables to the wok with the marinade and the stock. Bring to a boil, then simmer for 2 minutes or until the sauce has thickened. Stir in the toasted cashew nuts and chopped cilantro, and serve immediately with freshly cooked noodles.

Ingredients SERVES 4

1 lb. pork tenderloin
4 tbsp. soy sauce
1 tbsp. cornstarch
1 cup unsalted cashews
4 tbsp. sunflower oil
1 lb. leeks, trimmed and shredded
1-in. piece fresh root ginger, peeled
   and thinly sliced
2 garlic cloves, peeled and chopped
1 red bell pepper, deseeded
   and sliced
$1^1/_4$ cups chicken stock
2 tbsp. freshly chopped cilantro
freshly cooked noodles, to serve

Food fact

Now grown throughout the tropics, cashews originated in South America. The fruit is large and shiny, and pink, red, or yellow in color. It is sometimes made into a drink or jam. The small, hard-shelled, kidney-shaped seed in the center of the fruit contains the cashew nut.

Pork Chop Hotpot

1 Preheat the oven to 375°F. Trim the pork chops, removing any excess fat, wipe with a clean, damp cloth, then dust with a little flour and set aside. Cut the shallots in half if large. Chop the garlic and slice the sun-dried tomatoes.

2 Heat the olive oil in a large casserole dish and cook the pork chops for about 5 minutes, turning occasionally during cooking until browned all over. Using a slotted spoon, carefully lift out of the dish and set aside. Add the shallots and cook for 5 minutes, stirring occasionally.

3 Return the pork chops to the casserole dish, and sprinkle with the garlic and sun-dried tomatoes, then pour over the canned tomatoes with their juice.

4 Blend the red wine, stock, and tomato paste together, and add the chopped oregano. Season to taste with salt and pepper, then pour over the pork chops and bring to a gentle boil. Cover with a close-fitting lid and cook in the preheated oven for 1 hour or until the pork chops are tender. Adjust the seasoning to taste, sprinkle with a few oregano leaves, and serve immediately with potatoes and green beans.

Ingredients   SERVES 4

4 pork chops
flour, for dusting
1 cup shallots, peeled
2 garlic cloves, peeled
$1/_4$ cup sun-dried tomatoes
2 tbsp. olive oil
14oz. canned tomatoes
$2/_3$ cup red wine
$2/_3$ cup chicken stock
3 tbsp. tomato paste
2 tbsp. freshly chopped oregano
salt and freshly ground black pepper
fresh oregano leaves, to garnish

To serve:
freshly cooked new potatoes
fine green beans

Tasty tip
Choose bone-in chops for this recipe. Remove any excess fat and rind before cooking.

Lamb Pilaf

1 Preheat the oven to 275°F. Heat the oil in a flameproof casserole dish with a tight-fitting lid, and add the almonds. Cook, stirring often, for about 1 minute, until just browning. Add the onion, carrot, and celery, and cook gently for an additional 8–10 minutes until soft and lightly browned.

2 Increase the heat and add the lamb. Cook for an additional 5 minutes until the lamb has changed color. Add the ground cinnamon and chili flakes. Stir briefly before adding the tomatoes and orange zest.

3 Stir and add the rice, then the stock. Bring slowly to a boil and cover tightly. Transfer to the preheated oven and cook for 30–35 minutes until the rice is tender and the stock is absorbed.

4 Remove from the oven and leave for 5 minutes before stirring in the chives and cilantro. Season to taste with salt and pepper. Garnish with the lemon slices and sprigs of cilantro, and serve immediately.

Ingredients   SERVES 4

2 tbsp. vegetable oil
$^1/_4$ cup flaked or slivered almonds
1 medium onion, peeled and
    finely chopped
1 medium carrot, peeled and
    finely chopped
1 celery stalk, trimmed and
    finely chopped
$^3/_4$ lb. lean lamb, cut into chunks
$^1/_4$ tsp. ground cinnamon
$^1/_4$ tsp. chili flakes
2 large tomatoes, skinned, deseeded,
    and chopped
grated zest of 1 orange
2 cups easy-cook brown basmati rice
$2^1/_2$ cups vegetable or lamb stock
2 tbsp. freshly cut chives
3 tbsp. freshly chopped cilantro
salt and freshly ground black pepper

To garnish:
lemon slices
cilantro sprigs

Spicy Lamb in Yogurt Sauce

1 Blend the chili powder, cinnamon, curry powder, cumin, and seasoning with 2 tablespoons of the oil in a bowl, and set aside. Cut the lamb fillet into thin strips, add to the spice and oil mixture, and stir until coated thoroughly. Cover and allow to marinate in the refrigerator for at least 30 minutes.

2 Heat the wok, then pour in the remaining oil. When hot, add the cardamom pods and cloves, and stir-fry for 10 seconds. Add the onion, garlic, and ginger to the wok, and stir-fry for 3–4 minutes until softened.

3 Add the lamb with the marinading ingredients and stir-fry for an additional 3 minutes until cooked. Pour in the yogurt, stir thoroughly, and heat until piping hot. Sprinkle with the chopped cilantro and sliced scallions, then serve immediately with freshly cooked rice and pita bread.

Ingredients   SERVES 4

1 tsp. hot chili powder
1 tsp. ground cinnamon
1 tsp. medium hot curry powder
1 tsp. ground cumin
salt and freshly ground black pepper
2 tbsp. peanut oil
1-lb. lamb fillet, trimmed
4 cardamom pods, bruised
4 whole cloves
1 onion, peeled and finely sliced
2 garlic cloves, peeled and crushed
1-in. piece fresh ginger, peeled
   and grated
$^2/_3$ cup plain yogurt
1 tbsp. freshly chopped cilantro
2 scallions, trimmed and finely sliced

To serve:
freshly cooked rice
pita bread

Shepherd's Pie

1 Preheat the oven to 400°F about 15 minutes before cooking. Heat the oil in a large saucepan and add the onion, carrot, and celery. Cook over a medium heat for 8–10 minutes, until softened and starting to brown.

2 Add the thyme and cook briefly, then add the cooked lamb, wine, stock, and tomato paste. Season to taste with salt and pepper, and simmer gently for 25–30 minutes until reduced and thickened. Remove from the heat to cool slightly and season again.

3 Meanwhile, boil the potatoes in plenty of salted water for 12–15 minutes until tender. Drain and return to the saucepan over a low heat to dry out. Remove from the heat and add the butter, milk, and parsley. Mash until creamy, adding a little more milk if necessary. Season.

4 Transfer the lamb mixture to a shallow ovenproof dish. Spoon the mashed potatoes over the filling, spreading evenly to cover completely. Fork the surface, then cook in the preheated oven for 25–30 minutes until the potato topping is browned and the filling is piping hot. Garnish and serve.

Ingredients   SERVES 4

2 tbsp. vegetable or olive oil
1 onion, peeled and finely chopped
1 carrot, peeled and finely chopped
1 celery stalk, trimmed and
   finely chopped
1 tbsp. fresh thyme sprigs
5 cups finely chopped leftover
   roast lamb
$^2/_3$ cup red wine
$^2/_3$ cup lamb or vegetable stock
2 tbsp. tomato paste
salt and freshly ground black pepper
4 cups roughly chopped potatoes
2 tbsp. butter
6 tbsp. milk
1 tbsp. freshly chopped parsley
fresh herbs, to garnish

Tasty tip

A traditional shepherd's pie is always made from cold roast lamb, but you can make it with fresh ground lamb if desired. Simply fry 1 lb. lean meat in a nonstick skillet over a high heat until well browned, then follow the recipe.

Moroccan Penne

1 Preheat the oven to 400°F. Heat the sunflower oil in a large flameproof casserole dish. Add the chopped onion and fry for 5 minutes or until softened.

2 Using a mortar and pestle, pound the garlic, coriander seeds, cumin seeds, and grated nutmeg together into a paste. Add to the onion and cook for 3 minutes.

3 Add the ground lamb to the casserole and fry, stirring with a wooden spoon for 4–5 minutes until the meat has broken up and browned.

4 Add the eggplant to the meat and fry for 5 minutes. Stir in the chopped tomatoes and vegetable stock, and bring to a boil. Add the apricots and olives, then season well with salt and pepper. Return to a boil, lower the heat, and simmer for 15 minutes.

5 Add the penne to the casserole, stir well, then cover and place in the preheated oven. Cook for 10 minutes, then stir and return to the oven uncovered for an additional 15–20 minutes until the pasta is tender but still firm to the bite. Remove from the oven, sprinkle with toasted pine nuts, and serve immediately.

Ingredients   SERVES 4

1 tbsp. sunflower oil
1 red onion, peeled and chopped
2 garlic cloves, peeled and crushed
1 tbsp. coriander seeds
$^{1}/_{4}$ tsp. cumin seeds
$^{1}/_{4}$ tsp. freshly grated nutmeg
5 cups ground lean lamb
1 eggplant, trimmed and diced
14oz. canned chopped tomatoes
$1^{1}/_{4}$ cups vegetable stock
$^{1}/_{2}$ cup chopped dried apricots
12 ripe olives, pitted
salt and freshly ground black pepper
3 cups penne
1 tbsp. toasted pine nuts, to garnish

Helpful hint

Pine nuts are easy to toast. Sprinkle them on a foil-lined broiler pan and place under a medium broiler for 3–4 minutes, turning frequently until they are golden-brown. Or, fry them in a nonstick skillet, tossing every few seconds, as they can burn easily.

Shredded Beef in Hoisin Sauce

1 Trim the celery and peel the carrots, then cut into fine matchsticks and set aside.

2 Place the steak between 2 sheets of parchment paper. Beat the steak with a meat mallet or rolling pin until very thin, then slice into strips. Season the cornstarch with salt and pepper, and use to coat the steak. Set aside.

3 Heat a wok, add the oil and, when hot, add the scallions and cook for 1 minute, then add the steak and stir-fry for a further 3–4 minutes, until the meat is sealed.

4 Add the celery and carrot matchsticks to the wok, and stir-fry for an additional 2 minutes before adding the soy, hoisin, and chili sauces and the sherry. Bring to a boil, and simmer for 2–3 minutes until the steak is tender and the vegetables are cooked.

5 Plunge the fine egg noodles into boiling water and leave for 4 minutes. Drain, then spoon onto a large serving dish. Top with the cooked shredded steak, then sprinkle with chopped cilantro and serve immediately.

Ingredients   SERVES 4

2 celery stalks
3 medium carrots
1-lb. rump steak
2 tbsp. cornstarch
salt and freshly ground black pepper
2 tbsp. corn oil
4 scallions, trimmed and chopped
2 tbsp. light soy sauce
1 tbsp. hoisin sauce
1 tbsp. sweet chili sauce
2 tbsp. dry sherry
9-oz. package fine egg
    thread noodles
1 tbsp. freshly chopped cilantro

Tasty tip
Although this recipe calls for dry sherry, Chinese rice wine may be substituted if you have some on hand.

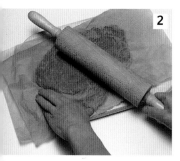

Spaghetti Bolognese

1 Heat the olive oil in a large heavy pan. Add the bacon and cook for 5 minutes or until slightly colored. Add the onion, carrot, celery, garlic, and bay leaf, and cook, stirring, for 8 minutes or until the vegetables are soft.

2 Add the ground beef to the pan and cook, stirring with a wooden spoon to break up any lumps in the meat, for 5–8 minutes until browned.

3 Stir the tomatoes and tomato paste into the meat and pour in the wine and stock. Bring to a boil, lower the heat, and simmer for a least 40 minutes, stirring occasionally. The longer you leave the sauce to cook, the more intense the flavor. Season to taste with salt and pepper, and remove the bay leaf.

4 Meanwhile, bring a large pan of lightly salted water to a rolling boil. Add the spaghetti and cook for about 8 minutes until tender but still firm to the bite. Drain and arrange on warmed serving plates. Top with the prepared Bolognese sauce and serve immediately, sprinkled with grated Parmesan cheese.

Ingredients   SERVES 4

3 tbsp. olive oil

$1/4$ cup chopped unsmoked bacon

1 small onion, peeled and
    finely chopped

1 carrot, peeled and finely chopped

1 celery stalk, trimmed and
    finely chopped

2 garlic cloves, peeled and crushed

1 bay leaf

$5^1/4$ cups ground beef

14oz. canned chopped tomatoes

2 tbsp. tomato paste

$2/3$ cup red wine

$2/3$ cup beef stock

salt and freshly ground black pepper

1 lb. spaghetti

freshly grated Parmesan cheese,
    to serve

Food fact

Bolognese sauce originated in the city of Bologna in Emilia-Romagna, where it is always served with tagliatelle, rather than spaghetti.

Pan-Fried Beef with Creamy Mushrooms

1. Cut the shallots in half if large, then chop the garlic. Heat the oil in a large skillet and cook the shallots for about 8 minutes, stirring occasionally, until almost softened. Add the garlic and beef, and cook for 8–10 minutes, turning once during cooking, until the meat is browned all over. Using a slotted spoon, transfer the beef to a plate and keep warm.

2. Rinse the tomatoes and cut into eighths. Wipe the mushrooms and slice. Add them to the skillet and cook for 5 minutes, stirring frequently, until the mushrooms have softened.

3. Pour in the brandy and heat through. Draw the skillet off the heat and ignite. Let the flames subside. Pour in the wine, return to the heat, and bring to a boil. Boil until reduced by one third. Draw the skillet off the heat, season to taste with salt and pepper, add the cream, and stir.

4. Arrange the beef on serving plates and spoon over the sauce. Serve with baby new potatoes and green beans.

Ingredients   SERVES 4

1 cup shallots, peeled
2 garlic cloves, peeled
2 tbsp. olive oil
4 medallions of beef
4 plum tomatoes
$1^3/_4$ cups mushrooms
3 tbsp. brandy
$^2/_3$ cup red wine
salt and freshly ground black pepper
4 tbsp. heavy cream

To serve:

new potatoes
freshly cooked green beans

Helpful hint

To prepare medallions of beef, buy a piece of fillet weighing approximately $1^1/_2$ lbs. Cut crosswise into four pieces.

Beef with Paprika

1 Beat the steak until very thin, then trim off and discard the fat and cut into thin strips. Season the flour with the salt, pepper, and paprika, then toss the steak in the flour until coated.

2 Meanwhile place the rice in a saucepan of boiling salted water, and simmer for 15 minutes until tender or according to the package directions. Drain the rice, then return to the saucepan, add ¹/₄ stick of the butter, cover and keep warm.

3 Heat the wok, then add the oil and ¹/₄ stick of the butter. When hot, stir-fry the meat for 3–5 minutes until sealed. Remove from the wok with a slotted spoon and set aside. Add the remaining butter to the wok and stir-fry the onion rings and button mushrooms for 3–4 minutes.

4 Add the sherry while the wok is very hot, then turn down the heat. Return the steak to the wok with the sour cream and seasoning to taste. Heat through until piping hot, then sprinkle with the cut chives. Garnish with bundles of chives, and serve immediately with the cooked rice.

Ingredients SERVES 4

1¹/₂-lb. rump steak
3 tbsp. all-purpose flour
salt and freshly ground black pepper
1 tbsp. paprika
1¹/₂ cups long-grain rice
6 tbsp. butter
1 tsp. oil
1 onion, peeled and thinly sliced
   into rings
2 cups wiped and sliced
   button mushrooms
2 tsp. dry sherry
²/₃ cup sour cream
2 tbsp. freshly cut chives
bundle chives, to garnish

Tasty tip

The button mushrooms in this recipe could be replaced by exotic or wild mushrooms. Chanterelles go particularly well with beef, as do porcini.

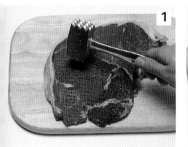

Desserts

We all love pudding! Everybody has room for some, so go on—
treat yourself. You don't have to slave away for hours to cook
up something sweet. Grape & Almond Layer is a quick and
scrumptious option, as is Apple & Cinnamon Brown Betty, and
there are plenty of dishes to delight the chocoholics out there:
does Chocolate Fudge Sundae or Iced Chocolate & Raspberry
Mousse sound good?

Grape & Almond Layer

1 Mix together the sour cream and yogurt in a bowl, and lightly fold in the sifted confectioners' sugar and the crème de cassis with a large metal spoon or rubber spatula until lightly blended.

2 Using a small knife, remove the seeds from the grapes, if necessary. Rinse lightly and pat dry on absorbent paper towels.

3 Place the seeded grapes in a bowl and stir in any juice from the grapes left over from seeding.

4 Place the Amaretto cookies in a plastic bag and crush coarsely with a rolling pin. Alternatively, use a food processor.

5 Cut the passion fruit in half, scoop out the seeds with a teaspoon, and set aside.

6 Divide the yogurt mixture among four tall glasses, then layer alternately with grapes, crushed cookies, and most of the passion fruit seeds. Top with the yogurt mixture and the remaining passion fruit seeds. Chill in the refrigerator for 1 hour and decorate with extra grapes. Lightly dust with confectioners' sugar and serve.

Ingredients   SERVES 4

1 cup reduced-fat sour cream
1 cup low-fat plain yogurt
3 tbsp. confectioners' sugar, sifted
2 tbsp. crème de cassis
1 lb. red grapes
2 cups Amaretto cookies
2 ripe passion fruit

To decorate:
confectioners' sugar
extra grapes (optional)

Food fact
Passion fruit is native to Brazil. They are purple in color and are about the size of an egg. Look for fruits that are wrinkled, not smooth. When wrinkled, they are ripe and at their best.

Crunchy Rhubarb Crisp

1 Preheat the oven to 350°F. Place the flour in a large bowl and cut the butter into cubes. Add to the flour and rub in with your fingertips until the mixture looks like fine bread crumbs, or blend for a few seconds in a food processor.

2 Stir in the rolled oats, brown sugar, sesame seeds, and cinnamon. Mix well and set aside.

3 Prepare the rhubarb by removing the thick ends of the stems and cut diagonally into 1-inch chunks. Wash thoroughly under cold running water and pat dry with a clean dishtowel. Place the rhubarb in a 1-quart casserole dish.

4 Sprinkle the sugar over the rhubarb and top with the crisp mixture. Level the top of the crisp so that all the fruit is well covered, and press down firmly. If desired, sprinkle a little extra granulated sugar on the top.

5 Place on a baking sheet and bake in the preheated oven for 40–50 minutes until the fruit is soft and the topping is golden brown. Sprinkle the pudding with some more granulated sugar and serve hot with custard or cream.

Ingredients   SERVES 6

1 cup all-purpose flour
4 tbsp. softened butter
$^2/_3$ cup rolled oats
4 tbsp. brown sugar
1 tbsp. sesame seeds
$^1/_2$ tsp. ground cinnamon
1 lb. fresh rhubarb
4 tbsp. granulated sugar
custard or cream, to serve

Tasty tip

To make homemade custard, pour $2^1/_2$ cups of milk with a few drops of vanilla extract into a saucepan and bring to a boil. Remove from the heat and let cool. Meanwhile, beat 5 egg yolks and 3 tablespoons of granulated sugar together in a mixing bowl until thick and pale in color. Add the milk, stir, and strain into a heavy saucepan. Cook on a low heat, stirring constantly until the consistency of heavy cream. Pour over the rhubarb crisp and serve.

Fruit Salad

1. Place the sugar and 1¹/₄ cups of water in a small saucepan and heat, gently stirring until the sugar has dissolved. Bring to a boil and simmer for 2 minutes. Once a syrup has formed, remove from the heat and allow to cool.

2. Using a sharp knife, cut away the skin from the oranges, then slice thickly. Cut each slice in half and place in a serving dish with the syrup and lychees.

3. Peel the mango, then cut into thick slices around each side of the pit. Discard the pit and cut the slices into bite-size pieces and add to the syrup.

4. Using a sharp knife again, carefully cut away the skin from the pineapple. Remove the central core using the knife or an apple corer, then cut the pineapple into segments and add to the syrup.

5. Peel the papaya, then cut in half and remove the seeds. Cut the flesh into chunks, slice the ginger into matchsticks, and add with the ginger syrup to the fruit in the syrup.

6. Halve the strawberries, add to the fruit with the cherries and almond extract, and chill in the refrigerator for 30 minutes. Sprinkle with mint leaves and lime zest to decorate, and serve.

Ingredients   SERVES 4

¹/₂ cup sugar
3 oranges
28 oz. canned lychees
1 small mango
1 small pineapple
1 papaya
4 pieces stem ginger, in syrup
4 tbsp. preserved ginger syrup
1 cup hulled strawberries
³/₄ cup cherries
¹/₂ tsp. almond extract

To decorate:

mint leaves
lime zest

Food fact

A fruit salad is the perfect end to a good meal because it refreshes the palate and is also packed full of vitamins.

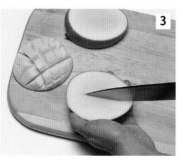

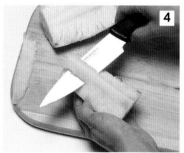

Lemon Surprise

1   Preheat the oven to 375°F. Lightly grease a deep ovenproof dish. Beat together the butter and sugar until pale and fluffy.

2   Add the egg yolks, one at a time, with 1 tablespoon of the flour, and beat well after each addition. Once added, stir in the remaining flour.

3   Stir in the milk, the lemon juice, and the orange juice.

4   Beat the egg whites until stiff, and fold into the dessert mixture with a metal spoon or rubber spatula until well combined. Pour into the prepared dish.

5   Stand the dish in a roasting pan and pour in just enough boiling water to come halfway up the sides of the dish.

6   Cook in the preheated oven for 45 minutes until well risen and spongy to the touch.

7   Remove the dessert from the oven and sprinkle with the confectioners' sugar. Decorate with the lemon twists and serve immediately with the strawberries.

Ingredients   SERVES 4

6 tbsp. reduced-fat butter
$^3/_4$ cup sugar
3 large eggs, separated
$^3/_4$ cup self-rising flour
2 cups low-fat milk
4 tbsp. lemon juice
3 tbsp. orange juice
2 tsp. confectioners' sugar
lemon twists, to decorate
sliced strawberries, to serve

Food fact

This recipe uses a bain-marie, (when the dish is placed in a pan as in Step 5), which enables the pudding to cook more slowly. This is necessary, as reduced-fat butter does not respond well when cooked at higher temperatures.

Baked Stuffed Amaretti Peaches

1 Preheat the oven to 350°F. Halve the peaches and remove the pits. Take a very thin slice from the bottom of each peach half so that it will sit flat on the baking sheet. Dip the peach halves in lemon juice and arrange on a baking sheet.

2 Crush the Amaretto cookies or macaroons lightly, and put into a large bowl. Add the almonds, pine nuts, sugar, lemon zest, and butter. Work with your fingertips until the mixture resembles coarse bread crumbs. Add the egg yolk and mix well.

3 Divide the Amaretto and nut mixture among the peach halves, pressing down lightly. Cook in the preheated oven for 15 minutes or until the peaches are tender and the filling is golden. Remove from the oven and drizzle with the honey.

4 Place 2 peach halves on each serving plate, and spoon over some sour cream or plain yogurt, then serve.

Ingredients
SERVES 4

4 ripe peaches
4 tbsp. butter
2 tbsp. lemon juice
$^3/_4$ cup Amaretto cookies
 or macaroons
$^1/_2$ cup toasted chopped blanched
 almonds
$^1/_2$ cup toasted pine nuts
3 tbsp. golden brown sugar,
 firmly packed
1 tbsp. grated lemon zest
1 large egg yolk
2 tsp. honey
sour cream or plain yogurt, to serve

Tasty tip

If fresh peaches are unavailable, use nectarines. Alternatively, use drained, canned peach halves that have been packed in juice, rather than syrup. You can vary the filling according to personal preference—try ground almonds, sugar, crumbled trifle sponge cakes, and lemon rind moistened with medium sherry.

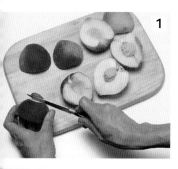
1

2

3

Apple & Cinnamon Brown Betty

1 Preheat the oven to 350°F. Lightly grease a 1-quart ovenproof dish. Peel, core, and slice the apples, and place in a saucepan with the granulated sugar, lemon zest, and 2 tablespoons of water. Simmer for 10–15 minutes until tender.

2 Mix the bread crumbs with the cinnamon and brown sugar. Place half the apples in the base of the prepared dish, and top with half of the crumb mixture. Place the remaining apples on top and cover with the rest of the crumb mixture.

3 Melt the butter and pour over the surface of the pudding. Cover the dish with nonstick parchment paper and bake in the preheated oven for 20 minutes. Remove the paper and bake for an additional 10–15 minutes until golden.

4 Meanwhile, make the custard by beating the egg yolks and sugar together until creamy. Mix 1 tablespoon of the milk with the cornstarch until a paste forms, and set aside.

5 Warm the rest of the milk until nearly boiling, and pour over the egg mixture with the paste and vanilla extract.

6 Place the bowl over a saucepan of gently simmering water. Stir over the heat until thickened and it can coat the back of a wooden spoon. Strain into a pitcher and serve hot over the pudding.

Ingredients SERVES 4

1 lb. apples
4 tbsp. granulated sugar
finely grated zest of 1 lemon
2 cups fresh white bread crumbs
$1/2$ tsp. ground cinnamon
$1/2$ cup brown sugar
2 tbsp. butter

For the custard:

3 large egg yolks
1 tbsp. granulated sugar
$2^1/2$ cups milk
1 tbsp. cornstarch
few drops vanilla extract

Tasty tip

For a richer, more luxurious custard, substitute the milk in this recipe for heavy cream and increase the number of egg yolks used to 4.

Almond & Pine Nut Tart

1 Preheat the oven to 400°F. Roll out the pastry, and use to line a 9-inch fluted flan pan. Chill in the refrigerator for 10 minutes, then line with waxed paper and dried beans, and bake blind in the preheated oven for 10 minutes. Remove the paper and beans, and cook for an additional 10–12 minutes until cooked. Allow to cool, then reduce the oven temperature to 375°F.

2 Grind the almonds in a food processor until fine. Add the sugar, salt, eggs, and vanilla and almond extracts, and blend. Add the butter, flour, and baking powder, and blend until smooth.

3 Spread a thick layer of the raspberry jelly over the cooled pastry shell, then pour in the almond filling. Sprinkle the pine nuts evenly over the top, and cook for 30 minutes until firm and browned.

4 Remove the pie from the oven and let cool. Dust generously with confectioners' sugar, and serve cut into wedges with whipped cream.

Ingredients SERVES 6

$1\frac{1}{4}$ cups sweet short-crust pastry
$\frac{3}{4}$ cup blanched almonds
$\frac{1}{2}$ cup sugar
pinch salt
2 large eggs
1 tsp. vanilla extract
2–3 drops almond extract
$\frac{1}{2}$ cup (1 stick) unsalted
butter, softened
2 tbsp. flour
$\frac{1}{2}$ tsp. baking powder
3–4 tbsp. raspberry jelly
$\frac{1}{2}$ cup pine nuts
confectioners' sugar, to decorate
whipped cream, to serve

Zabaglione with Marsala-Soaked Raisin Compote

1 Put the raisins in a small bowl with the lemon zest and ground cinnamon. Pour over the Marsala wine to cover, and leave to macerate for at least 1 hour. When the raisins are plump, lift out of the Marsala wine, and set the raisins and wine aside. Discard the lemon zest.

2 In a large heatproof bowl, mix together the egg yolks and sugar. Add the white wine and Marsala wine, and stir well to combine. Put the bowl over a saucepan of simmering water, ensuring that the bottom of the bowl does not touch the water. Beat constantly until the mixture doubles in bulk.

3 Remove from the heat and continue beating for about 5 minutes until the mixture has cooled slightly. Fold in the raisins and then immediately fold in the whipped cream. Spoon into dessert glasses or goblets, and serve with crisp cookies.

Ingredients
SERVES 6

2 tbsp. raisins

1 strip thinly pared lemon zest

$1/2$ tsp. ground cinnamon

3 tbsp. Marsala or Italian fortified wine

3 large egg yolks

3 tbsp. sugar

$1/2$ cup dry white wine

$1/2$ cup lightly whipped heavy cream

crisp cookies, to serve

Food fact
Zabaglione, an Italian concoction of eggs, sugar, and wine, is virtually identical to sabayon—the French dessert of eggs, sugar, and wine. Make the zabaglione as above, and omit the raisins. Serve with poached pears, summer fruits, or on its own in stemmed glasses.

Passion Fruit & Pomegranate Citrus Tart

1   Preheat the oven to 400°F. Sift the flour and salt into a large bowl, and rub in the butter until the mixture resembles fine bread crumbs. Stir in the sugar.

2   Whisk the egg yolk, and add to the dry ingredients. Mix well to form a smooth, pliable dough. Knead gently on a lightly floured surface until smooth. Wrap the pastry, and let rest in the refrigerator for 30 minutes.

3   Roll out the pastry on a lightly floured surface, and use to line a 10-in. loose-based tart pan. Line the pastry shell with waxed paper and dried beans. Brush the edges of the pastry with the egg white, and bake blind in the preheated oven for 15 minutes. Remove the paper and beans, and bake for 5 minutes. Remove, and reduce the oven temperature to 350°F.

4   Halve the passion fruit and spoon the flesh into a bowl. Whisk the sugar and eggs together in a bowl. When mixed thoroughly, stir in the heavy cream, the passion fruit juice and flesh, and the lime juice.

5   Pour the mixture into the pastry shell, and bake for 30–40 minutes until the filling is just set. Remove and cool slightly, then chill in the refrigerator for 1 hour. Cut the pomegranate in half and scoop the seeds into a sieve. Spoon the drained seeds over the tart, and dust with confectioners' sugar just before serving.

Ingredients   SERVES 4

For the pastry:

1$\frac{1}{2}$ cups all-purpose flour
pinch salt
$\frac{1}{2}$ cup (1 stick) butter
4 tsp. superfine sugar
1 small egg, separated

For the filling:

2 passion fruit
1 cup superfine sugar
4 extra-large eggs
$\frac{3}{4}$ cup heavy cream
3 tbsp. lime juice
1 pomegranate
confectioners' sugar, for dusting

Helpful hint

Pomegranates have a leathery skin and may be dark yellow to crimson in color. They have a distinctive, slightly acidic flavor.

1

2

4

Maple Pears with Pistachios & Simple Chocolate Sauce

1 Melt the butter in a wok over a medium heat until sizzling. Turn down the heat a little, add the pistachios, and stir-fry for 30 seconds.

2 Add the pears to the wok and continue cooking for about 2 minutes, turning frequently and carefully, until the nuts are beginning to brown and the pears are tender.

3 Add the lemon juice, ground ginger if using, and maple syrup. Cook for 3–4 minutes §until the syrup has reduced slightly. Spoon the pears and the syrup into a serving dish and let cool for 1–2 minutes while making the chocolate sauce.

4 Pour the cream and milk into the wok. Add the vanilla extract and heat just to boiling point. Remove the wok from the heat.

5 Add the chocolate to the wok and leave for 1 minute to melt, then stir until the chocolate is evenly mixed with the cream. Pour into a pitcher and serve with the pears while still warm.

Ingredients   SERVES 4

2 tbsp. unsalted butter
$^1/_2$ cup unsalted pistachios
4 medium-ripe firm pears, peeled, quartered, and cored
2 tsp. lemon juice
pinch ground ginger (optional)
6 tbsp. maple syrup

For the chocolate sauce:

$^1/_2$ cup heavy cream
2 tbsp. milk
$^1/_2$ tsp. vanilla extract
5 squares semisweet chocolate, broken into pieces and coarsely chopped

Food fact

Maple syrup is made by tapping maple trees in early spring when the sap is running. The thin, clear liquid is boiled until brown and syrupy. Most syrups are uniform in flavor and color, but it is possible to find syrups made in later spring, which have a richer flavor.

Orange Chocolate Cheesecake

1 Lightly grease and line an 8-inch round springform cake pan with nonstick parchment paper. Place the cookies in a plastic container, and crush using a rolling pin. Alternatively, use a food processor. Melt the butter in a medium-sized heavy saucepan, add the crumbs, and mix well. Press the crumb mixture into the bottom of the lined pan. Chill in the refrigerator for 20 minutes.

2 For the filling, allow the cream cheese to come to room temperature. Place the cream cheese in a bowl and beat until smooth, then set aside.

3 Pour 4 tablespoons of water into a small bowl and sprinkle over the gelatin. Allow to stand for 5 minutes until spongy. Place the bowl over a saucepan of simmering water and allow to dissolve, stirring occasionally. Let cool slightly. Melt the orange chocolate in a heatproof bowl set over a saucepan of simmering water, then let cool slightly.

4 Whip the cream until soft peaks form. Beat the gelatin and chocolate into the cream cheese. Fold in the cream. Spoon into the pan and level the surface. Chill in the refrigerator for 4 hours until set.

5 Remove the cheesecake from the pan and place on a serving plate. Top with the mixed fruits, dust with sifted confectioners' sugar, and decorate with sprigs of mint.

Ingredients   SERVES 8

8 graham crackers
4 tbsp. butter
4 cups mixed fruits, such as
    blueberries and raspberries
1 tbsp. confectioners' sugar, sifted
few fresh mint sprigs, to decorate

For the filling:

2 cups cream cheese
1 tbsp. gelatin
12 squares orange chocolate, broken
    into segments
2 cups heavy cream

Helpful hint

Always add gelatin to the mixture you are working with and beat well to evenly distribute it. Never add the mixture to the gelatin or it will tend to set in a lump.

Chocolate Fudge Sundae

1 To make the chocolate fudge sauce, place the chocolate and cream in a heavy saucepan and heat gently until the chocolate has melted into the cream. Stir until smooth. Mix the sugar with the flour and salt, then stir in sufficient chocolate mixture to make a smooth paste.

2 Gradually blend the remaining melted chocolate mixture into the paste, then pour into a clean saucepan. Cook over a low heat, stirring frequently until smooth and thick. Remove from the heat and add the butter and vanilla extract. Stir until smooth, then cool slightly.

3 To make the sundae, crush the raspberries lightly with a fork and set aside. Spoon a little of the chocolate sauce into the bottom of two sundae glasses. Add a layer of crushed raspberries, then a scoop each of vanilla and chocolate ice cream.

4 Top each one with a scoop of the vanilla ice cream. Pour over the sauce, sprinkle over the almonds, and serve with a wafer.

Ingredients   SERVES 2

For the chocolate fudge sauce:
3 squares semisweet chocolate, broken into pieces
2 cups heavy cream
$^{3}/_{4}$ cup granulated sugar
$^{1}/_{4}$ cup all-purpose flour
pinch salt
1 tbsp. unsalted butter
1 tsp. vanilla extract

For the sundae:
1 cup raspberries, fresh or thawed if frozen
3 scoops vanilla ice cream
3 scoops homemade chocolate ice cream
2 tbsp. toasted, slivered almonds
wafers, to serve

Helpful hint
Store any remaining fudge sauce in the refrigerator for 1–2 weeks, warming it just before serving.

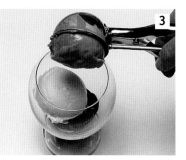

Iced Chocolate & Raspberry Mousse

1 Break the ladyfingers into small pieces and divide among four individual glass dishes. Blend together the orange juice and Grand Marnier, then drizzle evenly over the ladyfingers. Cover with plastic wrap and chill in the refrigerator for about 30 minutes.

2 Meanwhile, place the cream in a small, heavy saucepan and heat gently, stirring occasionally until boiling. Remove the saucepan from the heat, then add the pieces of semisweet chocolate and allow to stand untouched for about 7 minutes. Using a whisk, beat the chocolate and cream together until the chocolate has melted and is well blended and completely smooth. Let cool slightly.

3 Place the frozen raspberries and confectioners' sugar into a food processor or blender, and blend until coarsely crushed.

4 Fold the crushed raspberries into the cream and chocolate mixture and mix lightly until well blended. Spoon over the chilled ladyfingers. Lightly dust with a little unsweetened cocoa and decorate with whole raspberries, mint leaves, and grated white chocolate. Serve immediately.

Ingredients   SERVES 4

12 sponge ladyfingers
$1/_3$ cup orange juice
2 tbsp. Grand Marnier or orange-
    flavored liqueur
1 cup heavy cream
6 squares semisweet chocolate,
    broken into small pieces
2 cups frozen raspberries
6 tbsp. confectioners' sugar, sifted
unsweetened cocoa, for dusting

To decorate:

fresh whole raspberries
mint leaves
grated white chocolate

Helpful hint

Remove the raspberries from the freezer about 20 minutes before you puree them. This will soften them slightly, but they will still be frozen.

Chocolate Sponge Pudding with Fudge Sauce

1. Preheat the oven to 325°F. Grease a 1-quart casserole dish.

2. Cream the butter and the sugar together in a large bowl until light and fluffy.

3. Stir in the melted chocolate, flour, cocoa, and egg, and mix together. Turn into the prepared dish, and level the surface.

4. To make the fudge sauce, blend the brown sugar, cocoa, and pecans together, and sprinkle evenly over the top of the pudding.

5. Stir the granulated sugar into the hot coffee until it has dissolved. Carefully pour the coffee over the top of the pudding.

6. Bake in the preheated oven for 50–60 minutes until the top is firm to touch and there is a rich sauce underneath the sponge. Remove from the oven, dust with confectioners' sugar, and serve hot with crème fraîche.

Ingredients
SERVES 4

6 tbsp. butter
³/₄ cup granulated sugar
2 squares semisweet chocolate, melted
¹/₂ cup self-rising flour
3 tbsp. sweetened cocoa
1 extra-large egg
1 tbsp. confectioners' sugar, to dust
crème fraîche, to serve (if unavailable, use sour cream)

For the fudge sauce:
¹/₄ cup light brown sugar
1 tbsp. unsweetened cocoa
¹/₃ cup coarsely chopped pecans
2 tbsp. granulated sugar
1¹/₄ cups hot, strong, black coffee

Tasty tip
Try placing six halved and pitted fresh red plums in the base of the dish before adding the prepared chocolate sponge cake.

Index